OVERCOMER

OVERCOMER

8 WAYS TO LIVE A LIFE OF UNSTOPPABLE
STRENGTH, UNMOVABLE FAITH,
AND UNBELIEVABLE POWER

DR. DAVID JEREMIAH

W Publishing Group

An Imprint of Thomas Nelson

Published in Nashville, Tennessee, by W Publishing, an imprint of Thomas Nelson.

Published in association with Yates & Yates, www.yates2.com.

Thomas Nelson titles may be purchased in bulk for educational, business, fund-raising, or sales promotional use. For information, please email SpecialMarkets@ThomasNelson.com.

Unless otherwise noted, Scripture quotations are taken from the New King James Version®. © 1982 by Thomas Nelson. Used by permission. All rights reserved.

Scripture quotations marked NIV are taken from the Holy Bible, New International Version®, NIV®. Copyright © 1973, 1978, 1984, 2011 by Biblica, Inc.™ Used by permission of Zondervan. All rights reserved worldwide. www.Zondervan.com. The "NIV" and "New International Version" are trademarks registered in the United States Patent and Trademark Office by Biblica, Inc.™

Scripture quotations marked NLT are from the Holy Bible, New Living Translation. © 1996, 2004, 2007, 2013, 2015 by Tyndale House Foundation. Used by permission of Tyndale House Publishers, Inc., Carol Stream, Illinois 60188. All rights reserved.

Scripture quotations marked PHILLIPS are from The New Testament in Modern English by J. B. Phillips. Copyright © 1960, 1972 J. B. Phillips. Administered by the Archbishops' Council of the Church of England. Used by permission.

Scripture quotations marked NASB are from the New American Standard Bible®. Copyright © 1960, 1962, 1963, 1968, 1971, 1972, 1973, 1975, 1977, 1995 by The Lockman Foundation. Used by permission. (www.Lockman.org)

Scripture quotations marked KJV are from the King James Version. Public domain.

Any Internet addresses, phone numbers, or company or product information printed in this book are offered as a resource and are not intended in any way to be or to imply an endorsement by Thomas Nelson, nor does Thomas Nelson vouch for the existence, content, or services of these sites, phone numbers, companies, or products beyond the life of this book.

ISBN 978-0-7180-8320-5 (eBook)
ISBN 978-0-7852-2432-7 (IE)
ISBN 978-1-4041-0865-3 (Custom)

Library of Congress Control Number: 2018951094

ISBN 978-0-7180-7985-7

Printed in the United States of America
18 19 20 21 22   LSC   10 9 8 7 6 5 4 3 2 1

CONTENTS

Prologue   *vii*

Chapter 1: Overcomer   1

Chapter 2: Overcoming Weakness with Strength   21

Chapter 3: Overcoming Falsehood with Truth   41

Chapter 4: Overcoming Evil with Good   61

Chapter 5: Overcoming Anxiety with Peace   81

Chapter 6: Overcoming Fear with Faith   103

Chapter 7: Overcoming Confusion with Wisdom   123

Chapter 8: Overcoming Temptation with Scripture   141

Chapter 9: Overcoming Everything with Prayer   161

Chapter 10: Overcoming Death with Life   183

Acknowledgments   *203*

Notes   *207*

About the Author   *221*

PROLOGUE

It's hard out there. Sometimes it feels like the world is ripping apart at the seams. Sometimes it feels like your heart can't take any more hurt. But no matter what the world throws at you—anxiety, fear, confusion, temptation—you have a choice on how to respond.

You can concede defeat or live in the victory God promises you.

It's easy to say you choose victory, but are you ready to walk in it each day? Are you ready to win this fight against fear? Are you ready to overcome the world in practice and not just in theory?

In this book, I will show you how.

What would happen if you faced your challenges in the name of the Lord? What would life be like if your goal in every situation was to bring glory to His name? What would happen if you fully embraced God's strategy for victory?

If you did those things, you would be living as an Overcomer. And believe it or not, that's who you really are if you have placed your faith and hope in Christ: "Yet in all these things we are more than conquerors through Him who loved us" (Rom. 8:37).

This book teaches you God's strategy for overcoming the challenges you face. How do I know what that strategy is? Because when the Holy Spirit inspired Paul to list the spiritual armor we need to protect ourselves, he wrote:

Finally, my brethren, be strong in the Lord and in the power of His might. Put on the whole armor of God, that you may be able to stand against the wiles of the devil. For we do not wrestle against flesh and blood, but against principalities, against powers, against the rulers of the darkness of this age, against spiritual hosts of wickedness in the heavenly places. Therefore take up the whole armor of God, that you may be able to withstand in the evil day, and having done all, to stand.

Stand therefore, having girded your waist with truth, having put on the breastplate of righteousness, and having shod your feet with the preparation of the gospel of peace; above all, taking the shield of faith with which you will be able to quench all the fiery darts of the wicked one. And take the helmet of salvation, and the sword of the Spirit, which is the word of God; praying always with all prayer and supplication in the Spirit, being watchful to this end with all perseverance and supplication for all the saints. (Eph. 6:10–18)

Based on these verses, we know Satan attacks us in at least eight different ways:

- Satan wants to keep you from God's strength.
- He's after your honesty.
- He's after your heart and your righteous life.
- He wants to fill you with anxiety.
- He wants to fill you with doubt.
- He longs to confuse your mind.
- He loves to tempt you to sin.
- He hates it when you pray.

In each chapter of this book you'll learn an overcoming strategy to defeat these attacks. You'll meet men and women in these pages who overcame their own adversity, so you can learn from and be inspired by their determination.

You'll also discover the path to victory over the trials you face in your own life. Yes, all of them: loss, disappointment, betrayal, abuse, injury, lies, addiction, self-doubt, mistakes, grief, anger, anxiety, regret. There's nothing Satan can throw at you that you cannot overcome.

But the time to prepare is now. I cannot stress that enough.

When Satan attacks, you won't have time to google "spiritual armor." You won't have time to phone a friend for advice on a counterattack. You may not even have time to get down on your knees to pray.

You must be prepared.

In the first chapter, we'll focus on David, the Old Testament's greatest Overcomer. In the last chapter, I'll tell you the story of history's greatest Overcomer, the Lord Jesus Christ. And through the chapters in between, we'll discover eight strategies for overcoming the challenges we face in our lives:

- How to overcome weakness with strength
- How to overcome falsehood with truth
- How to overcome evil with good
- How to overcome anxiety with peace
- How to overcome fear with faith
- How to overcome confusion with wisdom
- How to overcome temptation with Scripture
- How to overcome everything with prayer

The journey of the Overcomer is a wonderful, profound, healing journey. God is all good, and He only gives good gifts—one after the other, again and again—to strengthen you for whatever the future holds. If you open your heart to receive those gifts, He will fill it to overflowing.

Living the life of an Overcomer will bring you strength, peace, courage, hope, and joy such as you've never known.

It will also bring victory in your spiritual life. That's important, my friend, because victory is God's purpose for His children: "Thanks be to God, who gives us the victory through our Lord Jesus Christ" (1 Cor. 15:57). "Thanks be to God who always leads us in triumph in Christ" (2 Cor. 2:14).

Join me on this journey to live a life of unstoppable strength, unmovable faith, and unbelievable power in the face of every challenge.

Join me and embrace your God-given destiny—for you are an Overcomer!

CHAPTER 1

OVERCOMER

You'd have to search long and hard to find a more unlikely hero than Desmond Doss, the real-life subject of the 2016 film *Hacksaw Ridge*. And you'd be equally hard-pressed to find a better representative for the theme of this book: how to live as an Overcomer.

Born in Virginia in 1919 to working-class parents, Doss volunteered for the army during World War II. Due to his deep religious conviction that God had called him to never carry a weapon, he trained as a medic and was assigned to a rifle company.

Imagine refusing to carry a weapon yet being determined to go to war! Doss's convictions earned him ridicule, abuse, and contempt from his fellow soldiers and disdain from his superiors, but he never wavered. Terry Benedict, who filmed a documentary about Doss in 2004, said, "He just didn't fit into the Army's model of what a good soldier would be."

But all that changed in April 1945, when Doss's company fought the Battle of Okinawa, the bloodiest battle of the Pacific war. The key to winning Okinawa was gaining a Japanese stronghold atop a four-hundred-foot sheer cliff the Americans called Hacksaw Ridge.

A bloody battle raged, but the Japanese held their ground. Finally, Doss's battalion was ordered to retreat.

But Doss could see American bodies strewn across the field, and he knew there were wounded among them. He stayed behind and, with machine gun and artillery fire bursting around him, ran repeatedly into the kill zone, carrying wounded GIs to the edge of the cliff and singlehandedly lowering them to safety in a makeshift rope gurney.

For twelve hours, he repeated this grueling task until he was sure no wounded American was left on the escarpment. By the time he finally left the ridge, Desmond Doss had saved the lives of seventy-five men!

Days later, the Americans took Hacksaw Ridge while Doss lay wounded in a base hospital. When his commanding officer brought him the precious charred and soggy Bible he'd lost in the initial assault, he was told every able man in the company—the same men who once ridiculed him for his faith—had insisted on searching for his Bible until it was found.

For his incredible feat, Doss was awarded the Congressional Medal of Honor.

Years later, he was asked how he found the strength to continue that night. His answer was simple. Each time he finished lowering another wounded man to safety down the cliff, he prayed, "Lord, just help me get one more."[1]

As Desmond Doss discovered, overcoming is a spiritual issue. But the idea of "overcoming" also has a military meaning: to conquer. As members of God's kingdom, we're called to conquer the barriers between who we are and who God wants us to be. Our goal is to "come over" from where we are today, and to flourish as the person God made us to be.

The obstacles we must overcome fall into three main categories: sin, the world, and the devil. Our own sinful nature is an obstacle; the temptations of the world are an obstacle; and the devil himself is an obstacle. Thankfully, in each case, God has equipped us to overcome every barrier in our path, as we'll discover starting in chapter 2.

In my estimation, David is the Old Testament's greatest Overcomer, and he is the poster child for the lessons we are about to learn. David fought a lot of battles during his life, but it's his first we all remember best—the day he defeated the giant Goliath.

In this first chapter of *Overcomer*, I invite you to take a fresh look at this well-known story. Listen to it as if you'd never heard it before, because I will use it to help you understand what it means to be an Overcomer. As you learn how David found the strength and courage to face down his giant, you'll discover how to overcome the challenges in your own life.

THE OVERCOMER'S CHALLENGE

In Israel today, there's a place where a deep ravine lies between two tall hills. This is believed to be the site where the battle between David and Goliath occurred.

On one hill was the army of Israel. On the other was the army of the Philistines. Down in the valley between them was a plain about one hundred yards wide—the length of a modern football field.

In the middle of that plain, between these two armies, stood a huge man named Goliath. And from the side of the Israelites came a teenage boy named David.

The story of David and Goliath in 1 Samuel 17 is not just a story about a boy fighting a giant. It's the conflict of the ages. It's the story of the battle that's raged since Satan first rebelled against God. The story of good versus evil; the challenge to the living God by the devil and his forces.

But first, how did these two unlikely opponents get there?

Let's start with Goliath.

The Bible specifically calls Goliath the champion of the Philistines and tells us he came from Gath, a well-known Old Testament city. Gath is the place the spies referred to when they returned to Moses with an evil report about the promised land. It was in Gath, according to the unbelieving spies, that giants existed—giants so huge that next to them they felt like grasshoppers.

One scholar claims that the portrayal of Goliath in 1 Samuel 17 is the most detailed physical description of any man found in Scripture.[2]

THE SIZE OF GOLIATH

"And a champion went out from the camp of the Philistines, named Goliath, from Gath, whose height was six cubits and a span" (1 Sam. 17:4).

During a time when the average man's height was about five feet tall, the measurements of Goliath are astounding. He stood "six cubits and a span," which means he was somewhere between nine foot six and nine foot nine.

That would make him at least two feet taller than the biggest players in professional basketball. And more than a foot taller than the tallest human alive today, Sultan Kösen, who measures eight feet three inches tall. But Goliath wasn't just tall and skinny. He was a huge man who probably weighed between four and five hundred pounds.

THE SIGHT OF GOLIATH

In his book *David and Goliath: Underdogs, Misfits, and the Art of Battling Giants*, author Malcolm Gladwell describes Goliath's armor in detail:

> To protect himself against blows to the body, he wore an elaborate tunic made up of hundreds of overlapping bronze fishlike scales. It covered his arms and reached to his knees and probably weighed more than a hundred pounds. He had bronze shin guards protecting

his legs, with attached bronze plates covering his feet. He wore a heavy metal helmet. He had three separate weapons, all optimized for close combat. He held a thrusting javelin made entirely of bronze, which was capable of penetrating a shield or even armor. He had a sword on his hip. And as his primary option, he carried a special kind of short-range spear with a metal shaft as "thick as a weaver's beam." . . .

Can you see why no Israelite would come forward to fight Goliath?[3]

To make matters worse, Goliath did not offer a one-time threat. Oh no. He came twice a day for six weeks, standing in the valley and shouting out his challenge every morning and every night.

THE SHOUT OF GOLIATH

Imagine this unnatural, huge beast of a man stomping to the middle of the plain in front of you and bellowing threats.

> Then [Goliath] stood and cried out to the armies of Israel, and said to them, "Why have you come out to line up for battle? Am I not a Philistine, and you the servants of Saul? Choose a man for yourselves, and let him come down to me. If he is able to fight with me and kill me, then we will be your servants. But if I prevail against him and kill him, then you shall be our servants and serve us." And the Philistine said, "I defy the armies of Israel this day; give me a man, that we may fight together." (vv. 8–10)

What does the voice of a man the size of Goliath sound like? A bellow to shake your soul, is what I imagine. A sound to strike terror into the hearts of the Israelites, as if his size hadn't already done that. He roared loud enough to be heard on both sides of a plain the size of football field, demanding that one man, just one, come and face him in single combat.

And not one man among the Israelites could bring himself to answer.

Single combat was a common practice in the ancient world. Rather than wipe out the enemy and lose all those potential servants, the Philistines preferred to settle their fights economically. Each side sent one man to fight, and those two men fought to the death. The winner's nation was declared victorious.

The loser's nation was enslaved, brutalized, and worse.

Who can blame the Israelites for not responding to Goliath's invitation? Their choice was certain death or certain slavery, and they all understood this. Who among us, doubting our skill and strength, lacking the power of the Lord, would want to be the man who faced that fate?

THE OVERCOMER'S CHARACTER

It was going to take some kind of warrior to confront Goliath. No one in King Saul's army was prepared to accept the job. But then, here came David.

David was the youngest of Jesse's eight sons. Although he had been anointed by the prophet Samuel as the next king of Israel, his time to rule had not yet come and he was still home with his family. Meanwhile, his three older brothers had followed Saul to the battle.

One day Jesse told David to go and check on his brothers, and to take them and their captain provisions. A wise father, Jesse not only wanted to ensure his sons had food, but also that their captain viewed them favorably. And, like any concerned father, he wanted news of how they were doing: "See how your brothers fare, and bring back news of them" (v. 18).

When his father sent him on this errand, it must have been thrilling for the boy to run off and see the armies. But, as excited as he was, he did something significant before he left that morning. He tended to his responsibilities and made sure someone would be caring for the sheep (v. 20).

That's an important point, a small but telling character trait. Overcomers concentrate on details that go unnoticed by others. They do what needs to be done, even when no one is watching.

THE CONVICTION OF DAVID

When David got to the camp, he dutifully found the supply master and gave him the supplies he'd brought. Then he ran to the army and greeted his brothers. As they were talking, Goliath strode out on the field below and shouted his challenge.

David seemed shocked that no one answered. He asked the men around him, "What shall be done for the man who kills this Philistine and takes away the reproach from Israel?" (v. 26). The soldiers answered that the king would give that man great riches, his daughter in marriage, and exempt his father's house from taxes.

That was quite an incentive.

While it was hard for David to understand why no one had taken up the call to defend Israel, it was even more appalling to David that Saul had not risen to the challenge himself. Saul stood head and shoulders above all his soldiers, and he was their king; he should have been the one to respond to Goliath's threat in the full power and strength of the Lord.

But Saul's relationship with God had deteriorated so much that he was operating in the flesh. He'd lost his ability to trust in the Living God.

So David volunteered!

THE COURAGE OF DAVID

Before David declared he would fight Goliath, something happened that reveals the human side of overcoming—a side that hasn't changed since biblical times. When David's oldest brother, Eliab, heard him asking about the reward, he was furious.

"Why did you come down here?" Eliab demanded. "And with whom have you left those few sheep in the wilderness? I know your pride and the insolence of your heart, for you have come down to see the battle" (v. 28).

David responded, "What have I done now? Is there not a cause?" (v. 29).

This was a brilliant answer. David both deflected Eliab's anger and brought the focus back to the matter at hand. "Don't be angry at me," he basically said. "Isn't there something more important for us to be thinking about?"

When a man or woman decides to be a champion for God, they set themselves up for a lot of heat and criticism. But like David, we can stand firm in our convictions when we are following the Lord and His calling.

THE CONFIDENCE OF DAVID

Then David declared that he would fight Goliath. Imagine the response! There must have been derision, laughter, and disbelief slowly turning to consternation and anger. Or would there have been awe? Surely some of the soldiers felt dread—both for the terrible fate this boy would face and for themselves, with what seemed to be their inevitable fate finally at hand.

When Saul heard of it, he summoned David. At first he tried to talk the boy out of it, reminding David of his youth and inexperience, and that Goliath was an experienced and trained warrior—"a man of war from his youth" (v. 33).

But David was steadfast. He knew his power was in the Lord. His courage was truly a product of his faith in God. Without God, David was powerless against that giant; but with God, he could overcome the fiercest man alive.

Unable to talk David out of the battle, Saul offered him his armor. But when David put it on, he couldn't walk. So, he took it all off. It was the king's own royal armor, surely the best in the whole army, but David knew he shouldn't wear it. If he couldn't walk, how could he fight?

THE OVERCOMER'S CONQUEST

Let's stop here and note that the three terms describing Goliath are all physical: size, sight, and shout. But the three terms describing David are all spiritual: conviction, courage, and confidence.

This is a key observation as we witness what happens next.

DAVID'S SLING

David headed for the plain. On the way, he stopped at a brook, gathered five smooth stones, and put them in his shepherd's pouch. With a sling in his hand, he approached Goliath.

It's worth taking a moment to understand the importance of the sling in biblical times:

> Ancient armies had three kinds of warriors. The first was cavalry—armed men on horseback or in chariots. The second was infantry—foot soldiers wearing armor and carrying swords and shields. The third were projectile warriors, or what today would be called artillery: archers and, most important, slingers. Slingers had a leather pouch attached on two sides by a long strand of rope. They would put a rock or a lead ball into the pouch, swing it around in increasingly wider and faster circles, and then release one end of the rope, hurling the rock forward.
>
> Slinging took an extraordinary amount of skill and practice. But in experienced hands, the sling was a devastating weapon. . . . In the Old Testament Book of Judges, slingers are described as being

accurate within a "hair's breadth." An experienced slinger could kill or seriously injure a target at a distance of up to two hundred yards. . . . Imagine standing in front of a Major League Baseball pitcher as he aims a baseball at your head. That's what facing a slinger was like—only what was being thrown was not a ball of cork and leather but a solid rock.[4]

DAVID'S STRATEGY

When Goliath saw David, he was insulted, even outraged.

"Am I a dog, that you come to me with sticks?" he said, and cursed David by his gods, probably using the name of Dagon, whom David knew to be a false god. This was an insult to the Living God of David.

Then Goliath goaded the boy even more. "Come to me, and I will give your flesh to the birds of the air and the beasts of the field!" (vv. 43–44).

Imagine what Goliath must have thought. He'd been coming to that valley every day for six weeks, waiting for somebody brave enough to meet him in battle, and all he ever saw were Israel's terrified soldiers. Then he saw a boy with no armor, no shield, and no sword.

Verse 42 says that Goliath "disdained" David, which literally means "he curled his lip."

David replied:

You come to me with a sword, with a spear, and with a javelin. But I come to you in the name of the LORD of hosts, the God of the armies of Israel, whom you have defied. This day the LORD will deliver you into my hand, and I will strike you and take your head from you. And this day I will give the carcasses of the camp of the Philistines to the birds of the air and the wild beasts of the earth, that all the earth may know that there is a God in Israel. Then all this assembly shall know that the LORD does not save with sword and spear; for the battle is the LORD's, and He will give you into our hands. (vv. 45–47)

This was the moment of truth. David had just infuriated the biggest bully on the block, and if God wasn't who David said He was, David would be history. David purposely intimidated Goliath, and in doing so set himself up to win the battle.

DAVID'S SHOT

At that, Goliath moved toward David. And that's when David ran *toward* the giant.

If you were watching from the hill, you'd have seen an enormous armed man start walking toward an apparently unarmed boy. Then you'd have seen something amazing: that boy running right toward the gigantic warrior!

This wasn't bravado. This was strategy. The giant wasn't going away, and David was determined to face him on his terms. So he ran to the point at which his sling's range was most effective. When he was where he wanted to be, he stopped running, quickly took a stone from his bag, and put it in the sling. Then, with years of experience and practice, he "slung it and struck the Philistine in his forehead, so that the stone sank into his forehead, and he fell on his face to the earth" (v. 49).

> Eitan Hirsch, a ballistics expert with the Israeli Defense Forces, recently did a series of calculations showing that a typical-size stone hurled by an expert slinger at a distance of thirty-five meters would have hit Goliath's head with a velocity of thirty-four meters per second [roughly seventy-six miles per hour]—more than enough to penetrate his skull and render him unconscious or dead.[5]

Then David made good on his promise. He ran and stood over Goliath, took the giant's own sword, and cut off the man's head with it.

The next few moments must have been filled with the shocked response of both sides. The Israelites probably thought, *Did I see what*

I thought I saw? And the Philistines knew they were in a world of trouble!

As Overcomers, when we reflect on this famous story, there are five lessons to be learned. Let's look at them one by one, through the lens of this story, and through the stories of others who faced similar giants—and defeated them.

When you're facing challenges . . .

REFUSE TO BE DISCOURAGED BY YOUR FRIENDS

Do you remember Eliab's reaction when he heard his youngest brother ask about Goliath? How many times has that happened to you? Have you ever determined to do something important, only to have your closest relatives or friends doubt you?

The sad fact is, we can't always count on those we look up to for support. In fact, sometimes all we can count on them doing is mocking or undermining us, instead of encouraging and standing behind us.

Whenever you want to do something great for God, get ready for your brothers and sisters to give you all the reasons why you'll fail. Often the criticism comes from those who don't have the courage to accept the challenge themselves. Their thinking seems to be that if they're not going to succeed, they don't want anyone else to either.

Be prepared for this challenge. Don't let the defensiveness, resentment, jealousy, or anger of others deflect you from your purpose. No matter how good your idea or goal is, don't expect others to immediately agree with your purpose or vision. You must be determined.

In the 1930s, Andrew Jackson Higgins ran a boat-building company in New Orleans. When America entered World War II, Higgins tried to convince the US Navy it needed a small landing craft with a flat bottom, high sides, and a front-opening portal to land troops in shallow waters that larger ships couldn't reach. But the navy had no interest.

At that point in the war, the focus was entirely on larger ships—battleships, cruisers, destroyers, and aircraft carriers. But Higgins was persistent. Finally, he convinced the navy brass of the need for such a craft, but they chose to design their own rather than give him the contract.

Higgins still refused to be discouraged. He prodded and nagged for two more years, until the navy reluctantly agreed to let him compete with their preferred contractors for the boat's design. Sure enough, Higgins's design was clearly superior. Finally, he was awarded the contract to build thousands of LCVPs (the acronym for Landing Craft, Vehicle, Personnel).

But the story doesn't end there. It ends three years later, on the beaches of Normandy.

We've all seen films of LCVPs being used as landing craft when allied troops crossed the English Channel and stormed the beaches of Normandy, ultimately liberating France and Western Europe from Nazi control. Those were Higgins's boats!

The Battle of Normandy would have been impossible without the shallow-draft boat. General Dwight D. Eisenhower said of Andrew Jackson Higgins, "He is the man who won the war for us."

Indeed, Higgins was an Overcomer.[6]

You may not realize it, but you know of so many others: Abraham Lincoln, raised poor and illiterate, was rebuffed by bankers, voters, employers, and law school deans before becoming president of the United States. Thomas Edison's teachers told him he was too dumb to learn anything—and he was fired from his first two jobs. Walt Disney was fired as a newspaper editor, with his boss saying he lacked imagination. Colonel Harland Sanders was told no 1,009 times by restaurant owners before he found one who'd try his now-famous fried chicken recipe.

Get the idea? Sometimes the biggest obstacles we face in life are the people around us, the people we need to convince to support us, or the people of little vision who need us the most.

And that brings us to the next lesson . . .

REINFORCE YOUR FOCUS ON GOD

Before he became the president of Child Evangelism Fellowship, Reese Kauffman was a successful manufacturer in Indianapolis. Some of the lessons he learned in business have helped him in every area of his life and ministry. One of those came in the shape of a canoe.

"One Friday afternoon I drove home in a state of depression," he said. "I lost four major accounts that week, customers I had worked hard to develop. Losing just one of them would have been a blow, but to lose all four in one week! I could see my business crashing down."

His wife, Linda, suggested he take the canoe out on the river awhile.

So I launched the canoe into the White River and started paddling upstream toward the bridge. As I paddled I talked to myself, asking myself questions and working through my emotions verbally.

Is God sovereign over my affairs? Yes. Does He love me? Yes, with a love beyond comprehension. Would God hurt me? No, He would never hurt me. He's my heavenly Father who works everything for my good. If those things are true, what am I worried about? I don't know.

As I thought through things from a heavenly or biblical perspective, the cloud lifted. My countenance changed and my joy returned. I turned the canoe around and returned to the house a different man. Later I realized the Lord was deleting some smaller accounts that weren't very profitable anyway. He cleared them out of my agenda to make room for larger and better accounts that were coming. I also realized afresh that it grieves the Lord when we don't trust Him. He has never once failed us. I can't tell you how many times both in business and in ministry I've had to metaphorically get back into that canoe and remind myself that whenever I am fretting it's because I'm not thinking biblically or seeing clearly.[7]

Kauffman learned to get his eyes off the "giant" in his life and onto the God over his life, just like David.

Max Lucado notes that David made only two observations about Goliath:

> One statement to Saul about Goliath (v. 36). And one to Goliath's face (v. 26, NIV). . . .
>
> That's it. Two Goliath-related comments (and tacky ones at that) and no questions. No inquiries about Goliath's skill, age, social standing, or IQ. David asks nothing about the weight of the spear, the size of the shield. . . . David gives no thought to the diplodocus on the hill. Zilch.
>
> But he gives much thought to God.[8]

Lucado goes on to list the nine times David referenced the Lord's strength: "God-thoughts outnumber Goliath-thoughts nine to two. How does this ratio compare with yours? Do you ponder God's grace four times as much as you ponder your guilt? Is your mental file of hope four times as thick as your mental file of dread? Are you four times as likely to describe the strength of God as you are the demands of your day?"[9]

It's all right to talk to God about your problems. But sometimes you need to talk to your problems about God. Preach the goodness of God to them. Prophesy the promises of God to them. Proclaim the victory of the cross to them.

Put your problems in perspective, and then . . .

REFLECT ON YOUR PREVIOUS VICTORIES

As king, Saul could have refused to allow David to fight Goliath. After all, there was a lot at stake. To convince Saul, David recalled his previous victories—not to brag, but to establish the truth.

> "Your servant used to keep his father's sheep, and when a lion or a bear came and took a lamb out of the flock, I went out after it and struck it, and delivered the lamb from its mouth; and when it arose against me, I caught it by its beard, and struck and killed it. Your servant has killed both lion and bear; and this uncircumcised Philistine will be like one of them, seeing he has defied the armies of the living God." Moreover David said, "The LORD, who delivered me from the paw of the lion and from the paw of the bear, He will deliver me from the hand of this Philistine." (vv. 34–37)

David didn't exclaim, "I can do it!" Instead, he noted that God had been on his side in the past, so he could trust God would be on his side in the present. He found courage in the Lord. His past victories gave him confidence in the power of God to win any challenge.

I like what I heard one time about testimonies: "If you have never had a test, you can never have a testimony." There are many ways to gather strength from your past successes, and to let them support your spirit and your faith.

When Jim Jones was five years old, he was shuttled from his family home in Mississippi to northern Michigan to live with his grandparents. The trauma of the move caused him to stutter. Hating school because other kids snickered when he spoke, he learned to speak as little as possible, consoling himself by writing poetry.

When Jim was a teenager, a new teacher came to the school—Donald Crouch, a devout Mennonite retired professor who loved poetry. Crouch found out Jim also loved poetry and wrote it. He urged the boy to read it aloud. Jim just shook his head and turned away.

But in class one morning, Crouch tricked him. The boy had turned in a poem he'd written, and the teacher said, "I don't think you wrote this."

When Jim, stuttering, insisted he had, Crouch forced him to prove it by reading it to the class. With his knees shaking while the other kids smirked and whispered, Jim began to read.

He found, as many who stutter have discovered, that the rhythms of poetry enabled his words to flow naturally. That day, Jim did not stutter. He continued to practice reading poetry and learned he had an excellent, resonant voice. After he graduated, he got his college degree, served in the army, and returned to study drama on the GI Bill.

Today we know Jim as James Earl Jones, a superb actor famous for his acting talent and for his sonorous, inimitable voice. Who can forget him as Darth Vader's voice in the original Star Wars films?

But again, that's not the end of the story. Years later, at the pinnacle of his career, Jones was asked to record the New Testament. He remembered Donald Crouch—the man who had given him victory over his disability all those years ago—and dedicated the reading to him.

As Jones put it, Crouch "not only helped to guide me to the author of the Scriptures, but as the father of my resurrected voice, also helped me find abundant life."[10]

This is one of the main reasons to record God's blessings in a journal. After all, life moves on, and we can forget our own successes and triumphs, as well as those who aided us. When you write down what God has done for you in the past, you are preparing yourself to believe Him in the future!

With that confidence in His faithfulness, you can . . .

RUN TOWARD YOUR PROBLEMS, NOT AWAY FROM THEM

In 2008, San Francisco architect Chris Downey experienced severe vision loss. Doctors discovered a tumor had wrapped itself around his optic nerve, requiring immediate surgery. When Chris awoke from anesthesia, his vision was blurry but at least he could see. Within days, however, everything went black. His eyesight was gone, and so was his job.

For most architects, going blind would be career-ending. But not for Chris Downey. Rather than allow his blindness to drive him from his calling, he faced it head-on. He found a blind computer scientist who'd developed a software program that printed blueprints on a tactile printer, letting him feel the lines on the paper.

After he learned to read blueprints through his fingertips, Chris's blindness gave him a unique way of visualizing spaces. As one architect explained it, Chris doesn't see the plans from above, as sighted people do. Instead, as he runs his fingers along the lines of a building's corridors, he visualizes the space as if he's walking through it. He's able to "see" obstacles and recommend efficiencies that sighted architects might overlook. Architectural firms hire Chris as a consultant to work on creating efficient designs that accommodate the blind.

Chris Downey didn't run away from his problem. Instead, he ran toward it with courage and creativity.[11]

Like Chris's problems, your problems probably don't go away by themselves. Instead, like Goliath challenging the Israelites, they keep showing up morning and evening, but often for a lot longer than forty days.

Whatever they are—family problems, workplace problems, financial problems—when you can't figure out the answers you may worry, get anxious, or lose sleep. For me, there are two times of day when problems are the most worrying: first thing in the morning and last thing at night.

That was the situation the Israelites faced. They were confronted morning and night with a challenge for which they had no answer. And how did David respond? "So it was, when the Philistine arose and came and drew near to meet David, that David hurried and ran toward the army to meet the Philistine" (v. 48).

So how do you overcome your problems? The story of David tells you how: Run toward your problems, embrace them, or confront them! Don't postpone them, ignore them, or try to work around them. Instead, face them head-on and deal with them!

Finally, as you are running toward your problem, be sure to . . .

REMEMBER FOR WHOM YOU ARE FIGHTING

In the autumn of 1964, Washington, DC, socialite Mary Pinchot Meyer was murdered execution-style along the canal where she walked daily. The police found Ray Crump Jr., a black day-laborer, nearby and arrested him for the murder. Two eyewitnesses claimed to have seen Crump standing over the victim's body. They described him as a black man, at least five foot eight and weighing about 185 pounds.

Washington defense attorneys shied away from the case, but Dovey Johnson Roundtree took it for a fee of one dollar. In court, federal prosecutors presented a tower of circumstantial evidence, including twenty-seven witnesses and more than fifty exhibits, to argue that Crump committed the murder.

But defense attorney Roundtree conducted her own extensive investigation and found major discrepancies in the prosecution's case. In the end, she presented only three witnesses and one exhibit. The exhibit was Crump himself, a frail, thin man barely five feet three inches tall. After only a twenty-minute summation, Roundtree won the case.

Why did Dovey Roundtree take such a high-profile, supposedly unwinnable case for which she received no compensation? The answer is that she knew she was taking on a cause larger than her client and even larger than herself.

Roundtree was the first black member of the Women's Bar

Association of the District of Columbia and a committed Christian. Throughout her lifetime, Roundtree took on cases that seemed hopeless because she believed in justice and knew for whom she was fighting: the God of justice.[12]

Do you know that in every situation you, too, can find the strength you need by remembering for whom you are fighting? David did. Listen to his words to Goliath: "You come to me with a sword, with a spear, and with a javelin. But I come to you in the name of the LORD of hosts. . . . All this assembly shall know that the LORD does not save with sword and spear; for the battle is the LORD's, and He will give you into our hands" (verses 45, 47).

What a difference it would make if we faced our challenges like David did. If we said, "Lord, for Your honor and glory, I'm going to do the right thing. I'm going to honor You and face my battles in the power of Your name."

In the next chapters, you'll find the strategy of the Overcomer explained and the path of the Overcomer laid out before you. You'll discover what happens when you remember for whom you are fighting.

But it will be up to you to follow it or not. Here is something that might help.

While change can be hard, new habits are most easily acquired when there's a great reward waiting for you. Well, I promise you there is no greater reward than the one that waits for you on the other side of this journey: "He who overcomes shall inherit all things" (Rev. 21:7).

You are called to be an Overcomer. You are called to walk in victory, strength, peace, and love. Come walk the path Paul laid out for you in the pages that follow.

It's time to begin your new life as an Overcomer!

For everyone born of God overcomes the world. This is
the victory that has overcome the world, even our faith.
—1 JOHN 5:4, NIV

CHAPTER 2

OVERCOMING WEAKNESS WITH STRENGTH

Canadian speed skater Denny Morrison won his first Olympic medal in 2006 and continued winning medals right through the 2014 Winter Olympics. After that, his eyes were firmly set on the 2018 Games in South Korea. But in May 2015, Morrison was in a horrific motorcycle accident and barely survived multiple serious injuries, including one that left him with a titanium rod in his leg.

As soon as possible, he began the arduous process of rehabilitation and training, still determined to qualify for the 2018 Olympics. But the next year, after he and his girlfriend, Josie Spence, completed a three-week bike trip, Spence noticed suspicious behavior in Morrison: slurred speech, droopy face, left-side weakness, and a left-foot flip-flop that kept falling off. Spence knew the signs. She rushed Morrison to a hospital where he was diagnosed as having had a stroke.

Again, Morrison recovered and dove back into training, now also struggling with the mental aftereffects of the stroke, including

21

depression. Remarkably, in 2017, he and Spence, also a Canadian speed skater, both qualified to represent Canada at the 2018 Winter Olympics.

Training for that level of competition pushes athletes to their limits, but Morrison's teammates repeatedly said he was their inspiration to keep going no matter what. His coach called him the most resilient person he'd seen. And, although Morrison didn't medal in 2018, his journey to get there was a victory in itself.

Describing his "grit" and determination, Morrison said, "It's human nature to encounter adversity and, when you do, there's a choice you have to make: Are you going to fight? Are you going to overcome and work toward your goals? Or are you going to give up and fail?

"When things stand in the way between you and what you want to achieve, it's that grit factor that gets you where you want to go. Goals don't come easy for anyone, no matter the line of work. But I think if you make a gritty attempt and push forward, you'll surprise yourself and everyone else with how far you can go."[1]

THE OVERCOMER'S STRENGTH

As Denny Morrison learned, strength comes in many forms. So does weakness. There's marital and moral weakness, financial and physical weakness, parental and job-related weakness. But the most debilitating weakness of all is weakness in your spiritual life—in your walk with God.

Suffering, challenges, and hardships are universal. At some point, we all face something that shakes us to the core. The cause can be external, such as injury, loss, or mistreatment by others. It can be internal, such as self-doubt, poor choices, inflated pride, or addictions. In our core passage in Ephesians, we're told to face all realities of an oppositional world with the strength we receive from our spiritual life.

As Paul was making his final appeal to the Ephesians, he wrote: "Finally, my brethren, be *strong* in the Lord and in the *power* of His *might*" (Eph. 6:10, emphasis added). In the Phillips translation we read, "be strong—not in yourselves but in the Lord, in the power of his boundless resource."

Paul's command to be strong echoes others throughout the Bible.

- When God commissioned Joshua as Moses's successor to lead the nation of Israel, He commanded him on three different occasions to "be strong and of good courage" (Josh. 1:6, 7, 9).
- David said to his son Solomon, "Be strong and of good courage, and do it; do not fear nor be dismayed, for the LORD God—my God—will be with you" (1 Chron. 28:20).
- Paul prepared Timothy for his new pastoral role with this counsel: "You therefore, my son, be strong in the grace that is in Christ Jesus" (2 Tim. 2:1).

In Scripture we see example after example of God coming alongside people who felt weak and inadequate—who felt the absence of the strength needed for the assignment they'd been given—and calling them to be strong. In fact, there are more than thirty occasions in the Bible where God *commands* someone to be strong.

When you read Paul's motivational words to the Ephesians, you might logically assume the command is to be strong in order to fight. After all, this passage describes how to equip yourself as a soldier, and fighting is what soldiers do. But read the passage more carefully and you discover that this is not a call to fight at all.

It is a call to *stand*.

Four times in Ephesians 6 the apostle Paul uses the language of standing to describe how to apply spiritual strength (vv. 11, 13, 14). Next to these verses in my Bible I've written: STRONG TO STAND.

Why aren't we commanded to fight? Because Christ, by His death and resurrection, has already defeated Satan. That's why we read verses in the Bible such as:

- "Yet in all these things we are more than conquerors through Him who loved us" (Rom. 8:37),
- "But thanks be to God, who gives us the victory through our Lord Jesus Christ" (1 Cor. 15:57), and
- "Now thanks be to God who always leads us in triumph in Christ" (2 Cor. 2:14).

From the spiritual perspective, we're not fighting *for* victory, but *from* victory, and this changes everything. We're called to be strong so we'll stand in the victory that's already been won. As we look back, we rest in Christ's victory over sin, Satan, and death. As we look forward, we face the future knowing God will always lead us in victory. This is what it means to be an Overcomer!

This is how Paul put it to the Corinthians: "Watch, stand fast in the faith, be brave, be strong" (1 Cor. 16:13).

STANDING STRONG

In the film version of J. R. R. Tolkien's *The Fellowship of the Ring*, actor Ian McKellen plays the role of the timeless wizard Gandalf the Grey. As he and the other members of the Fellowship of the Ring flee from Orcs through the Mines of Moria, beneath Mount Caradhras, they're pursued by a terrible and ancient monster called a Balrog. In the mines, they come to a deep chasm over which stretches a thin, stone bridge. Gandalf shoos the others across the bridge to safety and, standing in the middle of the bridge, turns to face his foe.

The Balrog is a demonic creature, a living manifestation of fire.

Fire erupts from his throat, fire emanates from his body, and fiery lashes whip back and forth around him. As the Balrog makes every attempt to destroy the wizard, Gandalf plants his feet on the stone bridge, faces the monster, raises his arms—staff in one hand, sword in the other—and bellows, "You shall not pass!"

You no doubt know how the story continues from there—and if you don't, I won't spoil the surprise. But here's my point: Gandalf the Grey fought by standing, not by swinging his sword or his staff. This is what Paul is telling you, that you are called by God to fight by standing firm, to take a stand so that evil shall not pass. Through your faith, He gives you the courage and strength to do this.

But what if your faith is weak? What if self-doubt, pain, or limiting beliefs are so loud in your head and heart they're all you hear?

I understand. Let's face it, we all look at Gandalf, and say, "Well, it was easy for him. That's who he was." And it's true, Gandalf was as well-equipped for this battle as possible. Also, his enemy was unmistakable—nobody would look at a Balrog and wonder if it was an enemy or not!

Our journey is different. We don't always have a clear purpose or destination. Our enemies are often well-disguised. And we don't live in a fictional place called Middle Earth, surrounded by beings with superhuman strength and ability.

Or do we?

I believe our world is very much a kind of "middle earth"—midway between Creation and Re-creation. We all face great challenges. The evil one flings "fiery darts" at us daily, to knock us off balance, or over the precipice. He does everything in his tremendous power to prevent us from achieving our eternal destination.

Each day you must ask yourself, as you lean on the strength of God: "Am I going to overcome and work toward my goals? Or am I going to give up and fail?"

Every morning, as your brain pulls itself from sleep and into the waking world, you make decisions. How will you start your day? How will you speak to and treat your spouse, your child, your colleague, the stranger next to you? Will you take steps to care for yourself, or will you give in to the rush of life and neglect your own needs?

And when you're attacked in a way that exposes your weakness, what will you do? Will you fight? (Satan is stronger than you.) Will you run? (He is faster than you.) Will you try to endure? (He is more patient than you.)

Or will you *stand*?

I urge you to take Paul's words and defend the ground of your life by standing firm. Fight by standing in the victory that is already yours in Jesus Christ. That's the only thing you have that your enemy doesn't have; it's the only thing for which he has no defense. Simply stand in the full power of God's strength through Jesus Christ.

FINDING THE STRENGTH YOU NEED

I've always been a high-energy person. When I was a boy my mother often said, "David Paul, where do you get all that energy?"—not in admiration, but in frustrated exhaustion.

In high school, I sang in the choir, played in the band, played baseball and basketball, and ran track. I went to college on a basketball scholarship, carried a full class load, and worked at two different radio stations during my junior and senior years.

While attending seminary in Dallas, I worked as a dockhand. Every weekend my wife, Donna, and I drove to Fort Worth to serve as interns at the Northwest Bible Church. Somehow, I managed to play basketball in an industrial league in my spare time.

After seminary, we moved to Haddon Heights, New Jersey, and served the youth of the Baptist church in a frenetic seven-day-a-week commitment. Two years later we followed the direction of the Lord to Fort Wayne, Indiana, where alongside seven families we planted the Blackhawk Baptist Church. Ask anyone who's started a church, and they'll probably tell you it's the hardest thing they've ever done. Donna and I would agree.

In 1981, I accepted the call to San Diego to take the reins of the church pastored by Dr. Tim LaHaye. But it wasn't just a church. It was also a primary and secondary school system. It was one church in three locations, and at that time serious plans were underway for a retirement center. I was involved in all of it, attending board and staff meetings and preaching five times every weekend. I always seemed to have the energy I needed for each assignment. I don't remember feeling tired because I never needed much sleep.

But on September 26, 1994, everything changed. I was diagnosed with stage four lymphoma and immediately went into a protocol of chemical treatment.

What I remember most was the weakness and profound fatigue the medicines inflicted on my system. No matter how much I slept, by 9:00 A.M. I wanted to go back to bed. I went from being a high-energy guy who never stopped, to being constantly fatigued, confused, and yes, frightened by this weakened state in which I found myself. Never before had I understood what it felt like to be weak.

On the first Sunday after completing the stem cell therapy that God used to cure me of cancer, I struggled to prepare myself to address our congregation for the first time in eight weeks. I was doing okay until our choir began singing the song "Total Praise," by Richard Smallwood. It wasn't the first time I'd heard that song, but on this day it affected me deeply. The words, which praise God for His strength, grabbed hold of my heart.

As I sat there on the front row, I began to cry. I knew God was the One who had strengthened me in my recovery from cancer. Almighty God was the source of my strength. He was the strength of my life.

This is the truth of Scripture. Our God is an awesome God—a God of ultimate strength.

- "The God of Israel is He who gives strength and power to His people. Blessed be God!" (Ps. 68:35).
- "Trust in the LORD forever, for in . . . the LORD is everlasting strength" (Isa. 26:4).

If God is your strength, and yet within you there is weakness, what do you do? Just believing what the Bible says about the might and power of God doesn't overcome weakness. The apostle James reminds us that "even the demons believe—and tremble!" (James 2:19).

The great truth is this: You don't have to beg God for strength, and you don't have to look for strength. God is looking to give His strength to those who need it and will receive it!

So how do we overcome our weakness with His strength?

Let me tell you the incredible truth I have learned: God has promised to *give* us His strength!

- "Have you not known? Have you not heard? The everlasting God, the LORD, the Creator of the ends of the earth, neither faints nor is weary. His understanding is unsearchable. *He gives power to the weak*, and to those who have no might He increases strength" (Isa. 40:28–29, emphasis added).
- "Fear not, for I am with you; be not dismayed, for I am your God. *I will strengthen you*, yes, I will help you, I will uphold you with My righteous right hand" (Isa. 41:10, emphasis added).

If you translate these promises from the Old Testament into the language of the New Testament, you hear the apostle Paul exalting, "I can do all things through Christ who strengthens me" (Phil. 4:13).

God has all the strength you'll ever need. And God desires to make His strength available to you. But how do you access that strength? How do you download God's strength into your life?

WE DOWNLOAD GOD'S STRENGTH FROM HIS WORD

Biblical scholar R. A. Torrey was once approached by a man who complained he got nothing out of Bible study. "Read it," Torrey said.

The man replied, "I do read it."

"Read it some more," said the man of God. "Take one book and read it twelve times a day for a month." He suggested the discouraged Christian start with 2 Peter because it contains only three chapters.

Later, the man said, "My wife and I read 2 Peter three or four times in the morning, two or three times at noon, and two or three times at dinner. Soon I was talking 2 Peter to everyone I met. It seemed as though the stars in the heavens were singing the story of 2 Peter. I read 2 Peter on my knees, marking passages with my colored pencils. Teardrops mingled with the colors, and I said to my wife, 'See how I have ruined this part of my Bible.'"

And his wife simply reminded him that as the pages of his Bible had gotten darker, his life had become lighter.[2]

That reminds me of something I heard years ago: "If your Bible is falling apart, it usually means that you are not."

The psalmist wrote, "My soul melts from heaviness; strengthen me according to Your word" (Ps. 119:28). But how do we open our hearts for God to do this?

Think of it this way: Your computer's hard drive contains all the applications you use for word processing, accounting, graphics, and more. When you launch one of those programs, the content of that application is "downloaded" from the hard drive into temporary memory where your computer's operating system finds it and delivers it to your computer's screen. Until that program is called on, it sits unused on the hard drive.

In other words, the program is just data waiting to solve a problem. You have to call on that data and apply it.

In a similar way, God's Word is filled with "great and precious promises" that "pertain to life and godliness" (2 Pet. 1:3–4). All the strength we need for the challenges of life is found in the Bible. A Bible sitting on a shelf is full of strength-giving truth, but that truth changes nothing until it's moved from the shelf into your heart and mind.

We access the power of God by reading, memorizing, listening to, meditating on, and obeying the Bible. Like loving words from an encouraging friend, the words you find in the pages of Scripture will strengthen your soul with wisdom, joy, and light (Ps. 19:7–8). They'll impart the certainty of God's Word to give you strength.

On November 19, 2007, Pauline Jacobi loaded her groceries into her car in the Walmart parking lot in Dyersburg, Tennessee. Then she got in the driver's seat to head home. Suddenly, a man jumped into the front seat beside her.

"I have a gun and I'll shoot if you don't give me money," he said.

The ninety-two-year-old Jacobi refused the demand three times before saying, "If you kill me, I'll go to heaven and you'll go to hell. Jesus is in this car, and he goes with me everywhere I go."

Tears welled in the man's eyes, and for the next ten minutes Jacobi ministered to him about faith, God, and eternity. Finally, he told her he would go home and pray. Jacobi responded that he could pray any time he wanted; God would hear him.

Then she reached into her purse and gave him all the money she had left—ten dollars. Tears rolled down his cheeks as he took the money and left, but not before leaning across the seat and kissing Jacobi on the cheek.[3]

What gave Pauline Jacobi the strength to verbally stand up to this man? It was the strength of her spiritual life, the strength of her love for Christ, and her confidence in His Word. And that strength was reinforced by her habit of reading the Bible every day, downloading the Word of God into her heart and mind. What a remarkable Overcomer!

WE DOWNLOAD GOD'S STRENGTH FROM WORSHIP

When your heart is caught up in the worship of God, something happens to you inwardly. Worship fills your heart with the worthiness of God and uplifts your spirit. That's why the Bible is filled with verses like these:

- "Be exalted, O Lord, in Your own strength! We will sing and praise Your power" (Ps. 21:13).
- "To You, O my Strength, I will sing praises; for God is my defense, my God of mercy" (Ps. 59:17).

One of my favorite Old Testament passages is from the book of Habakkuk. This book opens to us the heart of a prophet agonizing over God's inattention to his prayers. Habakkuk was watching his nation, Israel, fall into sin and rebellion. He couldn't understand why God didn't judge this nation, why God didn't even respond to his prayers. And then one day God answered Habakkuk and told him He planned to use the Chaldeans as the rod of judgment against the people of Israel.

At that time, the Chaldeans were the most wicked nation on the face of the earth. And yet God was going to use *them* to judge His chosen people?

The prophet Habakkuk was overwhelmed. Why would God do

such a thing? It went against everything he'd come to know and love about God. When you read this short book, you feel the agonizing pain of the imponderable situation in which Habakkuk found himself.

The first words of the third and final chapter of Habakkuk read as follows: "A prayer of Habakkuk the prophet, on Shigionoth." While the exact meaning of *shigionoth* is not known, it is generally believed to be some sort of musical instruction. Hold that thought and look at the last words in the book: "To the Chief Musician. With my stringed instruments." Those two musical inscriptions tell us that everything written between them is a song. And it's one of the most profound worship songs in the entire Bible, concluding with these haunting lines:

> Though the fig tree may not blossom,
> Nor fruit be on the vines;
> Though the labor of the olive may fail,
> And the fields yield no food;
> Though the flock may be cut off from the fold,
> And there be no herd in the stalls—
> Yet I will rejoice in the LORD,
> I will joy in the God of my salvation.
>
> The LORD God is my strength;
> He will make my feet like deer's feet,
> And He will make me walk on my high hills.
>
> —HABAKKUK 3:17–19

In the end, Habakkuk had to come to terms with this question: Will I trust in the wisdom and goodness of God no matter what happens around me?

Instead of looking back or looking around, Habakkuk decided to look up. And his conclusion became this amazing hymn of praise.

How do we follow Habakkuk's example? We worship the Lord. We simply love, adore, and praise God's name—no matter what's going on around us. We know He will march with us to the farthest corners of the earth and to the end of the age.

As we worship, our life comes together in unexpected ways. And as we face challenges head-on, we keep praising and worshiping the God who is greater and stronger than any challenge in our path. We overcome our weakness with strength downloaded through worship.

WE DOWNLOAD GOD'S STRENGTH BY WAITING

We might not like the act of waiting, but the Bible says when we wait on the Lord, we will find the strength we need:

- "Wait on the LORD; be of good courage, and He shall strengthen your heart; wait, I say, on the LORD!" (Ps. 27:14).
- "Even the youths shall faint and be weary, and the young men shall utterly fall, but those who wait on the LORD shall renew their strength" (Isa. 40:30–31).

The essence of waiting is to accept the unfolding of God's plan in His time. We're preparing ourselves to hear His still small voice when He knows we're ready. But waiting is the opposite of what our fast-paced world has taught us.

So—how do we wait on God?

SLOW DOWN

Take a moment and consider how the frantic pace of our lives affects the peace of our souls. The Bible, by precept and personal illustration, points us in a different direction. To download strength from God we need to make time to be with Him. We need to slow down, get quiet, and pray.

Isaiah said, "In quietness and confidence shall be your strength" (Isa. 30:15).

Isaiah's word for "quiet" means ceasing activity, rather than the cessation of noise. This is the message of Isaiah 30—God wanted His people to stop their frantic activity by which they were trying to solve their own problems. The whole chapter is filled with the people's striving, running here and there trying to get help, and building alliances with pagan neighbors. You can feel the stress and tension escalating as you read the chapter.

As our challenges mount, our fatal tendency is to exert more strength and get busier. But God says the way we gain strength is by retreating into the quietness of His presence and waiting upon Him.

I've tried it both ways. Sometimes I've tried to run to every colleague, read every book, recruit every ally—and I end up more stressed than when I started.

Other times I've gone to God at the outset and said, "Lord, these things are too much for me. I don't know what to do or how to handle them, and I'm simply coming to You. You're the God of my life. Calm my soul and strengthen me for what lies ahead." And that is when peace and strength have come.

GET QUIET

We're deluged daily with noise, distractions, technology, and the clamor of our culture. Sometimes in airports I'd like to sit quietly and read, but television monitors blare the news. In doctors' offices we have to put up with game shows shouting from the wall. In large cities the sounds of jackhammers, car horns, and sirens are unending. At home our televisions, laptops, tablets, and smartphones are constantly playing, beeping, and pinging alerts at us.

All the noise increases tension. The *Washington Post* recently carried the story of a bluebird that built her nest seventy-five yards from a loud natural gas compressor. As the weeks passed, her stress hormone levels became skewed and her health deteriorated. Her body simply broke down, and her hatchlings couldn't survive. When scientists later sampled her blood, they found the same physiological symptoms as those who suffer from post-traumatic stress disorder.[4]

The article went on to describe the debilitating effects of noise pollution on the natural environment around us. It's creating enormous stress on wildlife. And on us. Our world is blanketed by so much noise—loud, harsh, and unsettling—that our souls are chronically stressed.

If you want to strengthen your soul by attuning yourself to the voice of God through His Word and in prayer, learn to get quiet. In his time of greatest weakness, the prophet Elijah looked for God in the midst of a powerful wind, a great earthquake, and a flaming fire. But God's voice was not heard in any of those dramatic displays. It was only after the fireworks were over and the world got quiet that Elijah heard God's "still small voice"—the voice that gave him the strength and courage he needed (1 Kings 19:12).

In his book on leadership, Ken Blanchard says, "Solitude and silence give us some space to reform our innermost attitudes toward people and events. They take the world off our shoulders for a time and interrupt our habit of constantly managing things, of being in control, or thinking we are in control."[5]

PRAY

Prayer is a river through which God's strength flows into your life. Perhaps you're weak because you haven't slowed down enough to get quiet before the Lord and ask Him to strengthen your heart and soul. Here's a simple starting point in discovering the gifts of quietness and prayer: take the "Be Still" challenge.

Every day this month, find ten minutes during which you can sit quietly, read God's Word, and silently reflect on what He tells you in Scripture. Find the quietest spot you know and get into a comfortable position. Spend a minute or so inhaling and exhaling deeply, getting God's oxygen to the bottom of your lungs.

Make sure you've closed your laptop and silenced your phone and put it away. (While you can read the Bible from your phone, it's better to have a printed copy for this exercise.) Begin reading in Psalms, John, Philippians, or wherever you'd like, and read just a few verses. Read them aloud if you want. It's also helpful to underline any phrase that especially speaks to you.

End your quiet time with a simple prayer. If you're not sure how to ask God for strength, consider making David's prayers your own:

- "Have mercy on me, O LORD, for I am weak; O LORD, heal me, for my bones are troubled" (Ps. 6:2).
- "But You, O LORD, do not be far from Me; O My Strength, hasten to help Me!" (Ps. 22:19).

When you leave your quiet place, you'll be amazed at how much better you handle your day. Over time, your ten minutes may grow to twenty or thirty minutes, for you will soon find that your soul craves silence. It's the holy hush that lets you hear the still, small voice of God.

Slow down. Take time to wait. Find time to be alone. No noise. No phones. No people. And as you pray, let God wash away the stress and strain of each day.

WE DOWNLOAD GOD'S STRENGTH THROUGH WEAKNESS

When the apostle Paul called out for God to remove his affliction, God answered him, saying, "My grace is sufficient for you, for My strength is made perfect in weakness." This assurance enabled Paul to declare, "Therefore I take pleasure in infirmities, in reproaches, in needs, in persecutions, in distresses, for Christ's sake. For when I am weak, then I am strong" (2 Cor. 12:9–10).

At first glance, Paul's declaration seems to be a contradiction. How can weakness make one strong? But Paul understood how difficult circumstances in his life taught him a profound truth about God's method for strengthening His children.

Years ago, a TV commercial advertised a glue with the claim that when it repaired a broken object, the point of the repair would be stronger than any other part of the object. Under stress, it would break anywhere else before breaking the bond of the glue. That's what God did for Paul. He filled Paul's broken place with His own strength, so that Paul was stronger in his weak place than anywhere else.

"God does not need your strength," said Charles Spurgeon. "He has more than enough power of His own. He asks for your weakness: He has none of that Himself, and He is longing, therefore, to take your weakness, and use it as the instrument in His own mighty hand. Will you not yield your weakness to Him, and receive His strength?"[6]

At the end of his life, in a Roman prison and abandoned by his friends, the great apostle Paul could still say with confidence, "But the Lord stood with me and *strengthened* me, so that the message might be preached fully through me, and that all the Gentiles might hear" (2 Tim. 4:17, emphasis added).

"It is when believers are out of answers, confidence, and strength, with nowhere else to turn but to God that they are in a position to be most effective," says John MacArthur. "No one in the kingdom of God is too weak to experience God's power, but many are too confident in their own strength. Physical suffering, mental anguish, disappointment, unfulfillment, and failure squeeze the impurities out of believers' lives, making them pure channels through which God's power can flow."[7]

Because Paul knew firsthand that God's strength is revealed in weakness, he realized that it was especially at the cross of Christ that His power was demonstrated in its fullest. There, in the most humiliating of all forms of execution, Paul discovered the surpassing power of God. "We preach Christ crucified, to the Jews a stumbling block and to the Greeks foolishness, but to those who are called, both Jews and Greeks, Christ the power of God and the wisdom of God" (1 Cor. 1:23–24).

At the cross Christ identified with us in our sin—meaning, He identified with us in our weakness. It's our sin that makes us weak and vulnerable to eternal death. But as Paul wrote, "For though He was crucified in weakness, yet He lives by the power of God. For we also are weak in Him, but we shall live with Him by the power of God" (2 Cor. 13:4).

We who have received the benefit of that "weakness" Christ demonstrated on the cross know the power that resulted from it! By God's power Christ was raised up again, enabling us to live by the power of His resurrection. Our lives have been transformed! We have been set free from our sin!

This is the great strength Overcomers find in weakness.

TURN YOUR WEAKNESS
INTO HIS STRENGTH

For a concert violinist, strength is four finely tuned strings; the absence of a string would put most violinists in a position of weakness. But Israeli-American violinist Itzhak Perlman is not most violinists. And Perlman knows something about weakness to begin with. Afflicted with polio as a child, he wears braces on both legs and walks with the help of crutches. Getting on stage and seated for a concert is no small matter.

One evening in 1995, while performing with an orchestra in New York City, one of the strings on his violin broke and hung limp off the side of the instrument. The loud *Snap!* ricocheted through the hall; it was obvious to everyone what had just happened. The audience, as well as the conductor and orchestra, assumed they would pause the concert while Perlman repaired, or replaced, his instrument.

Instead, the great violinist closed his eyes for a moment while the audience waited in silence, then motioned to the conductor to begin the piece again. What would be impossible for all but a few human beings—playing a violin concert with four good strings—was translated into something perhaps no one else could have done: play the same concert with only three strings. As he played, in his mind Perlman was adjusting, recomposing, innovating, and performing on the fly, turning a position of weakness into a performance of strength.[8]

Itzhak Perlman's lifetime of familiarity with the violin allowed him to turn a moment of defeat into a masterful victory. Your goal is to develop the resources you need to adjust, recompose, innovate, and prevail when confronted with your own challenges. For the Christian, that means knowing the source of strength that allows that to happen.

As an Overcomer, your strength is in God, not yourself. Stopping the "concert" of your life is not an option when you feel weak or overwhelmed. But if you diligently open your heart to the Lord and ask for His strength, He will fill you with it! And in that way, through your faith, the Lord will use your weakness to make you strong.

Be of good courage, and He shall strengthen
your heart, all you who hope in the LORD.
—PSALM 31:24

CHAPTER 3

OVERCOMING FALSEHOOD
WITH TRUTH

Saturday, June 24, 1899, was a slow news day in Denver, Colorado. Four reporters from the four Denver newspapers were hanging about the Denver railroad station hoping to catch site of an incoming celebrity or hear some other gossip they could turn into a story for the Sunday edition of their papers. No such luck. They all retreated to the Oxford Hotel to commiserate over their problem in the hotel bar.

Then one of the reporters, Al Stevens, had a "Eureka!" moment. He would just invent a story and turn it in for publication as factual. The other reporters sensed a possibility, but they sensed it would have to be a foreign story that couldn't be easily verified. So they agreed: "A group of American engineers stopped over in Denver last night en route to China to submit a bid on tearing down the Great Wall!"

Another reporter from the group asked, "Why would China want to tear down their most famous national monument?" A few ideas and theories later, they all agreed: "They were doing it as an act of international goodwill—to signify a new openness to the world, and to invite new waves of foreign trade." According to their fake story, the Great Wall would be replaced by a 1,500-mile highway into the heartland of China.

Brilliant! All four reporters wrote up their version of the story and submitted it to their respective papers.

So the news story was told—or the hoax masquerading as a news story was told. All four Denver papers printed the story, which reportedly made its way even to Europe and China. People around the world believed the United States was sending an envoy to dismantle the Great Wall of China.[1]

A WORLD OF LIES

Perhaps no other temptation—or tempter—is as easy to embrace as a simple lie. What harm can it do? After all, it's just words. . . .

And that's where the slippery slope begins.

We see it all around us: telephone and email scammers, serial cheaters, dishonest coworkers or bosses, men who use women and vice versa, bullies and social media trolls, even family members who take advantage of our love and generosity.

Jesus said of Satan, "He . . . does not stand in the truth, because there is no truth in him" (John 8:44).

If you have an email account, you've probably received emails from a "Nigerian prince" seeking your assistance in a large financial transaction that will result in you receiving a fee of hundreds of thousands of dollars. Or perhaps you've received mail from a "high-ranking official" in the United States government informing you that you're owed a large sum of money. Or an email from a well-known billionaire who selected you to receive a generous one-time gift from his foundation.

Sound familiar? In each of these instances, all that's required to receive your financial windfall is for you to confirm your contact information and send in a "processing" or "transaction" fee.

Like countless other ways trusting people can be taken advantage of, these "advance fee scams"—the promise of sending a small amount of money to receive a larger amount in return—have been documented for hundreds of years. And they show no signs of stopping. Our task is to do our best to separate truth from fiction, and for that, we have to know what truth looks like.

But before we look outside ourselves for the perpetrators, let's examine our own hearts.

In their book *Freakonomics*, Steven D. Levitt and Stephen J. Dubner tell the story of an IRS officer named John Szilagyi. In the early 1980s, Szilagyi had completed enough random audits of other people's tax returns to know that many US citizens were inflating the number of their dependents so they'd receive a bigger refund at the end of the year.

Szilagyi decided that something needed to be done, and his solution was to require taxpayers to list their children's Social Security numbers. "Initially, there was a lot of resistance to the idea," said Szilagyi. "The answer I got was that it was too much like *1984*."

A few years later, however, Szilagyi's idea was revisited and passed into law for 1986. When the following year's tax returns came trickling in, he and the rest of the IRS were astounded: seven million dependents had suddenly disappeared![2]

Most of those who took advantage of the easy exemption for dependents probably didn't consider themselves liars. Or cheats. But that doesn't change the truth or the facts. No matter how much you dislike the IRS, or anyone you choose to deceive, a lie is still a lie.

It's easy to assume that a lie is a foreign thing to us—something that invades our lives, homes, and relationships from the outside. But be careful you don't make excuses for yourself that you wouldn't make for others. Make time to take inventory of your own actions and choices. Doing so will be a lesson in humility and the first step to understanding how you can be deceived by the emperor of lies.

THE BELT OF TRUTH

In our core passage from Ephesians 6, Paul's first instruction is to "stand therefore, having girded your waist with truth" (v. 14). It may seem strange that the belt or girdle is the first item of the Roman soldier's equipment that Paul mentions, since it wasn't a piece of armor at all. But the belt had a central function that was vital to most of the soldier's armor and weapons.

The soldier's basic attire was a tunic—a shirt-like garment that draped from shoulder to knee. Over this he wore metal torso armor and long, protective leather strips that hung from his waist to his lower thighs around his entire body. His belt was a band of wide, thick leather with loops and slots that clamped over these items. From it hung a sword, rope, ration sack, money sack, and darts. Everything the soldier needed in hand-to-hand combat was on his belt, right there at his fingertips.

When running, the soldier pulled up his tunic and tucked it in his belt, freeing his legs for speed and maneuverability. This was known as "girding one's loins."

While the belt had no offensive function of its own, it was the piece of equipment that essentially held everything else together, keeping the soldier ready for anything he might face.

Here's what this means for us today: truth is what fits us for the life of a Christian. Truth holds everything together and makes us ready. At the center of our lives we place "the truth [that] is in Jesus" (Eph. 4:21). And everything we do is drawn from that all-encompassing center.

When we know the truth and live the truth, we can access our weapons quickly and confidently, without fear that anything is out of place in our lives. "We have renounced the hidden things of shame, not walking in craftiness nor handling the word of God deceitfully, but by manifestation of the truth commending ourselves to every man's conscience in the sight of God" (2 Cor. 4:2). Truth gives us courage to stand against our enemy.

Why is truth to be our primary concern? Because the weapons of Satan's major attacks against believers are falsehood and deception. He is the great deceiver! This is how the Bible describes the devil: "When he speaks a lie, he speaks from his own resources, for he is a liar and the father of it" (John 8:44).

When we stand in the truth, we never speak from our own resources. We speak from the truth revealed to us through the Bible and the Holy Spirit. Speaking truth is not always comfortable. But it is always right.

Some years ago, a prominent Bible scholar was about to publish a book explaining how his research led him to a conclusion about the authorship of an Old Testament book. He knew his findings would upset the prevailing consensus of modern scholarship, and he dreaded the storm of criticism that would follow. But he went on to say, "There is a worse fate than being misunderstood; it is to be to truth a timid friend."[3]

As a soldier wearing the belt of truth, you need not be timid about standing strong in defense of God's reality. From that belt you draw all the resources you need to combat a culture that promotes falsehood and attacks truth.

WHAT IS TRUTH?

Almost two thousand years ago, a Roman governor asked a profound—and familiar—question of a Man who was about to be executed: "What is truth?" (John 18:38).

We have no way of knowing whether Pilate's question was a serious inquiry or a sarcastic expression of a weary mind. But we do know that minutes later he turned Jesus over to an angry crowd to be crucified.

R. C. Sproul wrote:

Pilate judged the Truth. He sentenced the Truth. He scourged the Truth. He mocked the Truth. He crucified the Truth.

The irony is that at the very moment he asked his question, "What is truth?" he was staring at the pure incarnation of Truth. The One who is the Truth had just said to him, "Everyone who is of the truth hears My voice."[4]

People have been asking Pilate's question—"What is truth?"—ever since. And, just like Pilate, they have missed the answer.

In March 2017, *Time* magazine displayed a timely cover that asked the question, "Is Truth Dead?" It was designed to mirror a famous cover from fifty years earlier, which asked, "Is God Dead?"

Speaking about those magazines, Brett McCracken noted, "These two covers, 50 years apart, tell an important story. Without God as an ultimate standard of truth, without 'objective' truth that is the same for everyone, all we have are 'truths' as interpreted by individuals."[5]

According to Os Guinness, truth is in trouble:

Truth in any objective or absolute sense, truth that is independent of the mind of the knower, no longer exists. . . .

A simple way to illustrate this lies in the story of the three baseball umpires debating their different philosophies of umpiring. "There's balls and there's strikes," says the first, "and *I call them the way they are.*"

"No!" exclaims the second umpire. "That's arrogant. There's balls and there's strikes and *I call them the way I see it.*"

"That's no better," says the third. "Why beat around the bush? Why not be realistic about what we do? There's balls and there's strikes and *they ain't nothing till I call them.*"

The first umpire represents the traditional view of truth—objective, independent of the mind of the knower, and there to be discovered. The second speaks for moderate relativism—truth "as each person sees it" according to his or her perspective and interpretation. And the third umpire bluntly expresses the radically relativist, or postmodern position—"truth" is not there to be discovered; it's for each of us to create for ourselves.[6]

In the final analysis, truth corresponds to the first umpire's position—to reality, to what actually *is.* That's why truth is found in God, the great I AM. The philosophical search for truth ends with God Himself.[7]

Do you remember the story of Joseph in Egypt, how he was falsely accused by Potiphar's wife and condemned to prison (Genesis 39)? He knew the truth of his innocence, and he knew God knew he was innocent. So in the face of the lies of people, Joseph committed himself to the truth of God, and his faith was vindicated.

That's not just a Bible story. The same thing happened to Anthony Ray Hinton, who served almost thirty years on death row in an Alabama prison for murders he did not commit. Falsely accused, falsely incarcerated, and turned down over and over by appeals courts, Anthony Hinton kept his faith in the God who he believed knew the truth—and he was eventually exonerated and released from prison in 2015. He told his story in *The Sun Does Shine: How I Found Life and Freedom on Death Row.*

How do you live under the weight of a lie when you know the truth? Here's how Anthony Hinton survived:

When every court was saying "no," I believed God was still saying yes. I had to somehow find that faith and reach deep down in my soul and believe in the teaching that my mother taught me as a young boy, that God can do everything but fail. He sits high, and he looks low. That's how I really survived that 30 years of pure hell. . . .

I can say that God might have put me in prison to save my life. He might have put me in prison for me to listen to him, in order to write [my] book, to help change people's hearts and souls and to help them understand what true forgiveness is all about, to understand what his true friendship is all about, to make people understand what the legal system is all about. I have to believe that God allowed me to go there in order to show me all of these things.[8]

GOD IS TRUTH

There is such a thing as truth, and the God of truth knows what it is: "His work is perfect . . . His ways are justice, a God of truth and without injustice" (Deut. 32:4).

God knows the answer to the question Pilate asked Jesus. We may not always recognize or understand how God chooses to act on or reveal to us His truth at any given moment in time. Even if it takes thirty years, as it did with Anthony Ray Hinton, our calling is to trust the God of truth.

When the Bible says, "In the beginning God" (Gen. 1:1), ultimate reality is defined. God is "the self-existent One; He is the Creator of all that exists; God is truth, and all truth is God's truth."[9] In the Bible, He is called "the God of truth" on several occasions.

The Father, the first person of the Trinity, is truth:

- "Into Your hand I commit my spirit; You have redeemed me, O Lord *God of truth*" (Ps. 31:5, emphasis added).

- "So that he who blesses himself in the earth shall bless himself in the *God of truth*; and he who swears in the earth shall swear by the *God of truth*" (Isa. 65:16, emphasis added).

And Jesus Christ, the second person of the Trinity who came from the Father, is "full of grace and truth" (John 1:14). Because He is God, Jesus is justified in His claim to be "the way, the truth, and the life" (John 14:6).

The Bible teaches that Jesus Christ was and is the communicator of truth, the witness to the truth, the origin of the truth, and the preacher of the truth. He *is* truth embodied. Christ is the final revelation of God to man. Truth is not a system or a philosophy; it's a Person. If you want to know the truth of God, you must come to know Christ, because He alone is truth.

Just like the first two persons of the Godhead, the Holy Spirit also is truth:

- "But when the Helper comes, whom I shall send to you from the Father, the Spirit of truth who proceeds from the Father, He will testify of Me" (John 15:26).
- "However, when He, the Spirit of truth, has come, He will guide you into all truth; for He will not speak on His own authority, but whatever He hears He will speak; and He will tell you things to come" (John 16:13).
- "It is the Spirit who bears witness, because the Spirit is truth" (1 John 5:6).

Truth is not some nebulous idea, a flexible concept, or a theoretical assumption; it is a solid, clearly defined, unalterable entity. It is ultimate reality, residing in the triune God of the universe, and it is not open to reevaluation or redefinition.

WE OVERCOME FALSEHOOD BY SEEKING THE TRUTH

We live in an age of relativism, situational ethics, and lies. But as we stand as truth-tellers in a world of falsehood, God does not leave us unprepared. He equips us with the belt of truth so we may be ready to combat deception. So how do we actually outfit ourselves with the belt of truth and overcome falsehood? The Bible tells us it all starts with seeking truth.

The psalmist did this by meditating on God's Word: "Let the proud be ashamed, for they treated me wrongfully with falsehood; but I will meditate on Your precepts" (Ps. 119:78).

To do battle with the enemy, the believer needs to know the truth about God, the truth about Christ, and the truth that is in this book we call the Bible. Here are two critical steps we can take to do just that.

STUDY THE TRUTH

To seek the truth we must begin by recommitting ourselves to an in-depth study of doctrine. Doctrine is the truth of the Word of God organized and categorized to give us clarity about the issues of life. It is systematized truth.

The more we know of the pieces of Scripture, the less we will puzzle about how to live our daily lives and how our lives fit into an overarching picture. Intimate knowledge of the Bible enables us to understand how every action and event has meaning in relation to other acts and events, whether on a personal or cosmic level. This is why it's imperative that Christians become conversant with the Bible.

I urge you to answer for yourself the question Stu Weber asks: "Are you involved in a regular, rigorous regimen of Bible study? If not, what in the world are you doing? . . . Your mind, your most critical weapon in battle, is braced by doctrine. Your soul is strengthened by biblical knowledge."[10]

If God's people will make the knowledge of God and His Word the pursuit of their Christian lives, Satan will be thwarted in his every effort to divide, deceive, and destroy.

To seek the truth, you must diligently search the Scriptures. The wonderful news is that our seeking after the truth will never be in vain. God has promised to reward us when we diligently seek Him (Heb. 11:6).

SUBMIT TO THE TRUTH

Last year I had the privilege of writing the foreword to *Not God Enough*, a new book by pastor and theologian J. D. Greear. My favorite chapter, "You Don't Get Your Own Personal Jesus," included this provocative passage:

> When God appeared to Moses, he declared, "I am who I am." "I am who I am" is not "I am whoever you want me to be."
>
> Can we imagine how offensive it must be to God when we attempt to reshape him according to our preferences? How would you like it if someone did that to you? . . .
>
> My guess is that you'd be offended. If we wouldn't like someone else doing that to us, why would we think it's OK to do that with God? Do we think that our idea of God is better than who he actually is?
>
> Have we forgotten who we are talking about?[11]

Counterfeit truth is never more on display than in the way we often hear people speak of God in today's world. "My God wants me to be rich." "The God I believe in would never send anyone to hell." "How dare your God claim to be the only way to heaven!"

It reminds us of a statement attributed to Voltaire: "God created man in His own image, and man has been trying to return the favor ever since."

God is not my God or your God; He is simply God. He has never changed, and He never will. It is God's desire to change us into His image, but we have neither the authority nor the ability to change God into our image. It is simply not our place to create a God who makes us feel good about the way we're doing life.

As believers, we're called to overcome falsehood with truth. We aren't called to make up truth but to submit to the truth that is found in God—and to never waver. Today more than ever before in history, James Russell Lowell's famous words ring true:

> Truth forever on the scaffold, Wrong forever on the throne—
> Yet that scaffold sways the future, and,
>> behind the dim unknown,
> Standeth God within the shadow, keeping
>> watch above his own.[12]

WE OVERCOME FALSEHOOD BY SPEAKING THE TRUTH

Between 1963 and 1974, Coach John Wooden led the UCLA men's basketball team to ten NCAA national championships—including seven championships in a row between 1966 and 1972. Though he died in 2010 at age ninety-nine, he remains a legend in his field. A basketball genius and a mentor and guide to his players, Wooden was more concerned about them learning how to live a good life than anything else. If they lived well, he said, they would play well.

Wooden's father-like coaching style seemed odd in the turbulent years during which he coached. Bill Walton, one of Wooden's players who went on to great success as a professional player, said this about his coach: "We thought he was nuts, but in all his preachings and teachings, everything he told us turned out to be true."[13]

"Everything he told us turned out to be true." Can the people in your life say that about you? Or have you bought into the cultural trend that expects the truth to be embellished, massaged, exaggerated, withheld, or reversed when it suits your situation?

Unfortunately, there's a sanctioned form of lying used by some to justify not telling the truth. It's called "spin." Spin is the recasting, reinterpretation, or revising of the truth to make it more palatable. The point is not to be truthful; it's to reinterpret facts as necessary to take the edge off the truth and make it more politically correct and less offensive for your own goals.

But in God's sight, spin is nothing short of lying, and it is not acceptable in His sight:

- "These six things the LORD hates, yes, seven are an abomination to Him: a proud look, a lying tongue, hands that shed innocent blood, a heart that devises wicked plans, feet that are swift in running to evil, a false witness who speaks lies, and one who sows discord among brethren" (Prov. 6:16–19).
- "Lying lips are an abomination to the LORD, but those who deal truthfully are His delight" (Prov. 12:22).
- "'These are the things you shall do: speak each man the truth to his neighbor; give judgment in your gates for truth, justice, and peace; let none of you think evil in your heart against your neighbor; and do not love a false oath. For all these are things that I hate,' says the LORD" (Zech. 8:16–17).

Our words, spoken or written, cannot be taken back. Once a lie is out there, it has a life of its own. Even if the effects can be stopped or reversed, the reputation of the liar is forever damaged.

OVERCOMERS SPEAK THE TRUTH BOLDLY

The apostle Paul wrote, "Therefore, putting away lying, 'Let each one of you speak truth with his neighbor'" (Eph. 4:25).

It's not easy to be an honest friend. But if you're lucky enough to have one or two, you know they're the friends you turn to when you need truth the most.

Pastor and author Chip Ingram wrote about four people who "loved me enough to tell me things about my life that no one else cared enough to say."[14] Each addressed a different part of his life: relationships, character, ministry, and giftedness.

- *Relationships:* When he'd been a Christian about a year, Chip began a relationship with a non-Christian girl. And the relationship was heading in a dangerous direction. An older Christian friend took him aside and shared scriptures with him about being "unequally yoked" (2 Cor. 6:14–18) with unbelievers. Chip didn't like what he was hearing, of course, but after praying about it, he realized his friend had probably saved him from a great deal of trouble.

- *Character:* During college, when Chip was involved in a campus ministry, one of the leaders came to him to share some scriptures and talk about his pride. The leader was concerned that Chip's motivation seemed to be more to impress others than to please the Lord. Again, after prayer, Chip realized that his team leader's words were painful but true.

- *Ministry:* When Chip began pastoring a small rural church that was growing under his ministry, a long-time member warned him about letting church politics influence what he preached. He'd gotten subtle pressure from some members about his emphasis on preaching the truths of God's Word. Chip reevaluated his priorities and knew he had to stand firm regardless of the consequences.

- *Giftedness:* After Chip and his wife participated in a leadership development seminar, they met with one of the leaders. He had glowing things to say about how Chip's wife was using her gifts, but to Chip he said, "You're lazy. . . . You're a lazy preacher. . . . You're not doing near with your gift what you could be doing." Chip went home and changed his whole approach to his preaching ministry, putting in more time in diligent preparation and evaluation.[15]

Those four people changed the course of Chip's life. They were living illustrations of Proverbs 27:5–6: "Open rebuke is better than love carefully concealed. Faithful are the wounds of a friend, but the kisses of an enemy are deceitful."

OVERCOMERS SPEAK THE TRUTH LOVINGLY

Not only are we to speak truthfully, but we are to speak the truth "in love" (Eph. 4:15).

A fourth-grade teacher recovering from surgery received a get-well card from her class. It read, "Dear Mrs. Fisher, your fourth-grade class wishes you a speedy recovery by a vote of 15 to 14." I don't know if this story is true (probably not), but it hits only one of Paul's two admonitions in Ephesians 4:15: truth and love. The kids spoke the truth with a pinch of love when they wished their teacher a speedy recovery. But reporting the tally of the votes? Not so much.

In John 13:35, Jesus said, "By this all will know that you are My disciples, if you have love for one another."

Our words and actions must be clothed with love. Truth delivered harshly, judgmentally, unkindly, unsympathetically, or without knowing all the facts or context will likely not be heard or appreciated.

Kathleen LeBlanc shared an experience she had while playing Scrabble with a ninety-three-year-old woman in a local care home. It illustrates how words spoken in a loving manner can overcome falsehood and bring life:

> After our game, she outright asked me, "What do you think of doctor-assisted suicide?" and pointed to an article from the paper on the topic. I told her that I felt it was very sad that anyone should feel the need to take their life, and it's our failure as a society when anyone is left feeling this way. After some time discussing this, she expressed to me that she can sympathize with people who don't feel they have a reason to live in their suffering, as she too, often wonders why God still has her "stuck in this wheelchair."
>
> With tears in my eyes, I was able to tell her what a joy she is to me, and that I look forward to visiting her every week. She teared up as well, shock in her eyes, and said, "Really? Is that true?" I nodded, unable to get more words out. "Well then, perhaps there is reason enough for me to be here."[16]

WE OVERCOME FALSEHOOD BY LIVING THE TRUTH

Our Lord illustrated the power of truth in the way He lived His life. When Jesus' enemies came to arrest Him, He said to them, "Which of you convicts Me of sin?" (John 8:46). Nobody said a word. Do you know why? Because they did not have anything they could say. They had nothing legitimate to convict Him of because He was absolutely everything He had claimed to be.

When Jesus went to the cross, the centurion overseeing the execution said, "Truly this Man was the Son of God!" (Mark 15:39). How did he figure that out? He simply watched Jesus die as He had lived, exhibiting attributes that only the Son of God could possess. He saw Christ living the truth.

And the thief who hung on the cross next to Jesus said, "This Man has done nothing wrong" (Luke 23:41). Why would he say that? He too saw the truth exhibited in Christ even under the stress of such horrendous circumstances.

The Overcomer must be clothed with truthfulness not only proclaimed, but also integrated into his or her life. Listen to the words of the apostle John: "I have no greater joy than to hear that my children walk in truth" (3 John v. 4).

To walk in the truth means living out the biblical tenets of the Christian faith. It means, as the saying goes, ensuring our walk matches our talk. To help us do that, the Lord has given us two practices: confession and correction.

IT TAKES CONFESSION TO LIVE THE TRUTH

The first step to living the truth is to be honest about where you really are in life and in your walk with God. In John Ortberg's book *The Me I Want to Be*, he talks about the healing that comes from confessing our deepest secrets to a trustworthy and loving person:

> One of the most important moments of my spiritual life was when I sat down with a longtime friend and said, "I don't want to have any secrets anymore." I told him everything I was most ashamed of. . . . I told him about my jealousies, my cowardice, how I hurt my wife with my anger. I told him about my history with money and my history with sex. I told him about deceit and regrets that keep me up at night. I felt vulnerable because I was afraid that I was going to lose connection with him. Much to my surprise, he did not even look away.
>
> I will never forget his next words.
>
> "John," he said. "I have never loved you more than I love you

right now." The very truth about me that I thought would drive him away became a bond that drew us closer together. He then went on to speak with me about secrets he had been carrying.[17]

God desires for us to be whole, to know and love the truth at the very core of our being: "Behold, You desire truth in the inward parts, and in the hidden part You will make me to know wisdom" (Ps. 51:6). One of the ways we come to experience this wholeness is through confession. As James wrote, "Confess your trespasses to one another, and pray for one another, that you may be healed" (James 5:16).

IT TAKES CORRECTION TO LIVE THE TRUTH

To overcome falsehood and be fully aligned with the truth, we must ask the Holy Spirit to convict us of sin and lead us in righteousness. This is what David did in his prayer recorded in Psalm 139: "Search me, O God, and know my heart; try me, and know my anxieties; and see if there is any wicked way in me, and lead me in the way everlasting" (vv. 23–24).

Why did David pray that prayer? Because he realized that sin in his life could make him unfit for the responsibility he had been given. He wanted God to shine the light of truth into his life. He asked God to identify any wickedness that was in his life and lead him on a different path.

The theological word for what David was describing is *repentance*. It means to correct the way you are living and thinking. True repentance opens the door for you to walk into a new life, and when you step into this new world God shuts the door on the mistakes and sins of your past. Your task is to learn from those mistakes, to use them to transform your life. Often, this happens quickly at first, and in big ways. Over time, it can be more subtle. Repentance is a lifelong process.

Author and pastor Mark Buchanan explains:

Almost weekly, I ask people to repent. . . . I invite them to see things God's way. To align themselves, stem to stern, with God's purposes. Initially that alignment is violent and dramatic, a 180-degree turn. But thereafter it's mostly course corrections; 15 degrees here, 5 degrees there.

But every turn, by whatever degree, is good news. Every turn moves us closer to where we want to be.[18]

Almighty God wants sincere believers who face up to the sin in their lives and then face it down through confession and repentance. This is the way an Overcomer learns to live the truth.

TURN UP THE VOLUME ON TRUTH

One of the vivid memories of my growing-up years took place in a little village in Indiana called Winona Lake. This was the home of the Winona Lake Conference Grounds, and during the fifties and sixties it was a major conference center for evangelical Christians.

During that time my father was working on a graduate degree at the Winona Lake School of Theology. Every summer he took our whole family to Winona Lake for several weeks.

One of the groups that gathered in Winona Lake each year was Youth for Christ, at that time a huge and growing nationwide organization. One summer Youth for Christ invited Dr. Billy Graham to speak at their event. The little village was transformed into a media center as thousands of people came to see the celebrated evangelist.

Dr. Graham was to speak in the Billy Sunday Tabernacle, a throwback sawdust-trail pavilion—yes, there was actually sawdust on the floor. The pavilion seated more than 7,500 people on hard wooden benches. The huge windows were flung open to allow the lake breeze to cool the building and let people outside see what was going on inside. On this night, people stood twelve deep all around the tabernacle. Every seat inside and every spot where someone could stand was occupied for hours before the event.

A friend of mine operated the follow spotlight from the roof. He invited me to join him for the night, and that's how I ended up having one of the best places in the house to watch this dynamic young evangelist.

I don't remember the details of Billy Graham's message that night, but I do remember he preached the truth: that Jesus Christ is the only hope for lost mankind. When he gave the invitation, scores of people, young and old, came forward to receive Jesus Christ as their Savior. I never really recovered from that moment.

Billy Graham was a truth-teller, the greatest preacher of the gospel message in modern-day history. He opened the door for all of us who have used the power of radio and television for the purpose of preaching the truth to the masses.

As I was finishing this chapter, Billy Graham died. He was ninety-nine years old, and for over seventy years he dominated the evangelical landscape. My wife, Donna, and I attended his funeral held under a gigantic tent in Charlotte, North Carolina. As I sat there surrounded by almost every evangelical leader I'd ever met, I felt a great sadness—a great sense of loss.

This megaphone for the gospel had been silenced by death. And then I thought, *It's true that the megaphone has been silenced—there will never be another Billy Graham. But there are thousands of microphones still left. I cannot be a megaphone, but I can be a microphone for the truth of the gospel.*

On that day in Charlotte, I made a commitment to turn up the volume on telling the truth of the gospel. I challenge you to do the same.

You shall know the truth, and the truth shall make you free.
—JOHN 8:32

CHAPTER 4

OVERCOMING EVIL WITH GOOD

It was shocking news in 2017—a medical doctor and athletic trainer at Michigan State University was charged with sexually assaulting 150 female athletes, mostly gymnasts. After lengthy court appearances and trials, the doctor was found guilty and sentenced to up to 175 years in prison. The court proceedings were extended for days as the victims read impact statements to the court—their testimonies of what this man had done to them.

The words of these young female athletes were heart-wrenching. Anger and resentment flowed as freely as tears. As the women spoke about what happened to them, a growing awareness of the evil this doctor embodied pervaded the courtroom. What he did could not be described in any other way.

The last of the impact statements was read on January 24, 2018, by a young gymnast named Rachael Denhollander. She was the first of the athletes to come forward and accuse the team physician of sexual assault. It seemed fitting that she should have the final word in the courtroom. From a portion of her six-thousand word statement spoken directly to Larry Nassar, here is how Rachael determined to turn this terrible evil into something good:

Throughout this process, I have clung to a quote by C. S. Lewis, where he says, my argument against God was that the universe seems so cruel and unjust. But how did I get this idea of just, unjust? A man does not call a line crooked unless he first has some idea of straight. What was I comparing the universe to when I called it unjust?

Larry, I can call what you did evil and wicked because it was. And I know it was evil and wicked because the straight line exists. The straight line is not measured based on your perception or anyone else's perception, and this means I can speak the truth about my abuse without minimization or mitigation. And I can call it evil because I know what goodness is. And this is why I pity you. Because when a person loses the ability to define good and evil, when they cannot define evil, they can no longer define and enjoy what is truly good.[1]

Wow. Such poise and grace. That, more than anything I have recently read, is an illustration and demonstration of what it means to overcome evil with good. This young woman discovered how to overcome two kinds of evil: the evil of revenge within herself and the evil that was done to her. Rachael Denhollander is an Overcomer!

What enables someone to overcome evil with good in this way? How do we keep ourselves from succumbing to anger, bitterness, grief, and the desire for revenge? How do we keep our hearts from storing the residue of evil done to us or to those we love?

Let's look at the instruction Paul gave the Ephesian believers when he told them, using the metaphor of a Roman soldier, to "put on the breastplate of righteousness" (Eph. 6:14).

The breastplate of the common Roman soldier was a piece of armor made of hardened, reinforced leather. For an officer, the leather was covered with metal plating for extra protection. The breastplate covered the torso and protected the soldier's vital organs—especially his heart. A warrior without his breastplate was vulnerable and dangerously exposed to the enemy.

In his letter, Paul used this literal breastplate that protected the physical heart as a metaphor. Righteousness, he inferred, acts as a "breastplate" to protect the figurative, spiritual heart of the Christian—the spiritual center of one's life.

Righteousness is an old-fashioned word. *Merriam-Webster* defines it as acting in accord with divine or moral law, being free from guilt or sin, and being morally right or justifiable, as in a righteous decision.[2]

It is by appropriating the righteousness of Jesus Christ—His moral perfection and sinless life of obedience to the Father—and living righteously that we are able to overcome the evil that is within us and the evil that is around us.

HOW WE OVERCOME THE EVIL WITHIN US

When we think about overcoming evil with good, we tend to focus on the evil outside of us. But as the Russian writer Aleksandr Solzhenitsyn said, "If only it were all so simple! If only there were evil people somewhere insidiously committing evil deeds, and it were necessary only to separate them from the rest of us and destroy them. But the line dividing good and evil cuts through the heart of every human being."[3]

Solzhenitsyn was merely echoing Jesus, who pulled no punches when describing the evil in the human heart: "From within, out of the heart of men, proceed evil thoughts, adulteries, fornications, murders, thefts, covetousness, wickedness, deceit, lewdness, an evil eye, blasphemy, pride, foolishness. All these evil things come from within and defile a man" (Mark 7:21–23).

It's a depressing list, isn't it? And it's not even complete. There's no way to list all the evil humans can conceive. So before we try to confront the evil outside us, we need to examine the evil within. The unrestrained, unconverted human heart is capable of evil of every sort. And every man and every woman has the seeds of this evil growing in his or her heart.

Every single one.

The Bible says, "There is none righteous, no, not one; there is none who understands; there is none who seeks after God. They have all turned aside; they have together become unprofitable; there is none who does good, no, not one" (Rom. 3:10–12).

In his book *The Divine Intruder*, James Edwards points out how villains of world literature are always larger than life and often way more interesting than heroes. We're drawn to villains because we recognize them. Authors are able to write them as more believable and imitable because they are—we innately know these characters. We may not act out their pernicious ways, but we understand those ways without thinking.[4]

One of the most dangerous thoughts a human being, even a Christian, can have is, *Oh, I would never do something that evil!* That thought reveals a sad naïveté about one's own heart and a dangerous potentiality concerning the future.

So how do we overcome the evil within us? We can't. But Christ can.

THE OVERCOMER'S RIGHTEOUSNESS

The bad news is that we all have evil inside us. The good news is that Christ, in His goodness and mercy, overcame that evil for us by dying on the cross and then offering us His righteousness—a free gift that can only be received by faith. By His death and resurrection, Christ defeated all the "principalities . . . powers . . . rulers of the darkness . . . [and] spiritual hosts of wickedness" (Eph. 6:12). "And having disarmed the powers and authorities, he made a public spectacle of them, triumphing over them by the cross" (Col. 2:15 NIV).

Evil no longer has power over the one who is clothed with the righteousness of Christ.

The transaction of the cross is the most wonderful truth of the Bible. Here in twenty-three words, Paul gives us that message: "For [God] made [Christ] who knew no sin to be sin for us, that we might become the righteousness of God in Him" (2 Cor. 5:21).

When Jesus died on the cross, He took on our identity as a sinner. When we believe in Him we take on His identity as the righteous Son of God. By this transactional death, Jesus accomplished two critical things. First, He took our sin upon Himself; He became sin for us. Second, when we put our trust in Jesus, He not only forgives our sin, He gives His righteousness to us. We receive this righteousness the moment we believe that Jesus is the Son of God, repent of our sin, and ask for forgiveness.

Pastor Erwin Lutzer has given us a good illustration of how evil is overcome in the heart of the Christian:

> Imagine a book entitled *The Life and Times of Jesus Christ*. It contains all the perfections of Christ: the works He did, His holy obedience, His purity, His right motives. A beautiful book indeed.
>
> Then imagine another book, *The Life and Times of [insert your name]*. It contains all of [your] sins, immorality, broken promises, and betrayal of friends. It would contain sinful thoughts, mixed motives, and acts of disobedience.
>
> Finally, imagine Christ taking both books and stripping them of their covers. Then He takes the contents of His own book and slips it between the covers of [your] book. We pick up the book to examine it. The title reads, *The Life and Times of [insert your name]*. We open the book and turn the pages and find no sins listed. All that we see is a long list of perfections, obedience, moral purity, and perfect love. The book is so beautiful that even God adores it.[5]

That is how to overcome the evil within your heart! Put your trust in Christ and He does the rest.

Having received the righteousness of Christ by faith, we can now put on His righteousness in practice. We can take on the obligation and determination to live as closely to God's Word, and as closely to Jesus' example, as we are able. If we live this way, our heart is unburdened. It sings with love and joy, and is filled with the inexpressible wonder of Christ's love for us.

That is the kind of heart that can overcome evil.

HOW WE OVERCOME THE EVIL AROUND US

When Chris Carrier was ten years old, a stranger approached him, professing to be a friend of the boy's father. He needed Chris's help in picking out a Christmas present for his dad. So Chris climbed into the man's motor home.

A short time later the man pulled the vehicle into a field and stabbed Chris in the back of the neck. He then drove the vehicle, with the wounded boy inside, down a dirt road. He shot the boy in the left temple and dumped him by the side of the road in the alligator-infested Florida Everglades.

For six days, Chris lay there, in and out of consciousness, until he was found by a passing motorist. Miraculously, he survived his injuries but lost the ability to see out of his left eye. The police were never able to identify or find the attacker.

Chris lived in fear for the next three years until, at a church event, he heard the gospel and gave his life to Christ. He grew in his faith and decided to go into full-time ministry to help others find the peace and healing he had found in Jesus.

Many years later—Chris was now married with a family—a detective contacted Chris, saying an elderly man had confessed to the brutal crime. The man had a grudge against Chris's father and took out his anger against Chris as a way of hurting the boy's father. Chris visited the seventy-seven-year-old man, who was now broken and weak, in a nursing home. At first the man denied knowing anything about the crime, but eventually he apologized to Chris. Chris explained how he had become a Christian and how God had used that terrible event in his life to share God's forgiveness and love with many other people.

Chris's family began making almost daily visits to the nursing home, sharing the love of God with the man. And one Sunday afternoon, Chris's attacker received both God's and Chris's forgiveness and placed his faith in Christ. A few days later he died peacefully in his sleep.[6]

That is a powerful example of how one man overcame the evil around him. First, Chris allowed Christ to remove the notion of revenge from his heart. Then he overpowered the evil in his assailant's life by an outpouring of God's love.

The Bible gives clear direction on how we can do this, beginning with the central New Testament passage of Romans 12:17–21:

> Repay no one evil for evil. Have regard for good things in the sight of all men. If it is possible, as much as depends on you, live peaceably with all men. Beloved, do not avenge yourselves, but rather give place to wrath; for it is written, "Vengeance is Mine, I will repay," says the Lord. Therefore
>
> "If your enemy is hungry, feed him;
> If he is thirsty, give him a drink;
> For in so doing you will heap coals of fire on his head."
>
> Do not be overcome by evil, but overcome evil with good.

Here we find six ways to overcome evil with good—beginning with how to dispense with vengeance.

LEAVE VENGEANCE TO GOD

Paul wrote, "Repay no one evil for evil. . . . Beloved, do not avenge yourselves . . . for it is written, 'Vengeance is Mine, I will repay' says the Lord" (Rom. 12:17, 19).

Have you noticed the way we talk about getting revenge? We say we want to "get even," which means we want to even out the balance sheet. We want the person who has done evil *to us* to experience the same amount of evil *from us*. In other words, whatever you do, don't let anybody get ahead of you in doing evil—keep the scales perfectly balanced.

Pastor Charles Swindoll tells about a preacher who refused to take revenge. He once said to a person who hurt him, "I'm not going to get even. I'm going to tell God on you!"[7] Fortunately, we don't have to tell God anything; He knows and sees everything, including every act of evil. And He tells us that He will balance the scales one day.

But many people are not willing to wait for that day. They'll go to any lengths to balance the scales on their own.

For example, Nick Stafford of Cedar Bluff, Virginia, was upset with the county DMV office because they wouldn't give him access to their direct phone lines. So when it came time to pay the taxes on two cars he purchased, Nick brought to their office five wheelbarrows loaded with over 300,000 pennies to cover the assessment. His rationale: "If they were going to inconvenience me then I was going to inconvenience them."[8]

Similarly, in a 1991 baseball game between the Chicago Cubs and the Cincinnati Reds, Cubs outfielder Andre Dawson objected strenuously to a called strike by umpire Joe West. In the heated dispute that followed, Dawson bumped West (he claimed it was accidental) and was ejected from the game and fined $1,000. But Dawson got his revenge by making it publicly known that on the check he sent to pay the fine he'd written, "Donation for the blind."[9]

When we attempt to take vengeance on another person, we're

usurping that role from God. God says vengeance is His, and we have no right or authority to take on a role He reserves for Himself. The Bible tells us explicitly: "You shall not take vengeance, nor bear any grudge against the children of your people, but you shall love your neighbor as yourself: I am the LORD" (Lev. 19:18).

This is the verse Christ quoted in Mark 12:31 when He affirmed that to "love your neighbor as yourself" is the second greatest commandment in all Scripture. By the time of Christ's ministry, this commandment had been corrupted by the development of a new Jewish tradition: love your neighbor and hate your enemies. This tradition condoned executing vengeance on anyone who harmed you.

But Christ corrected that distortion of Leviticus 19:18 in the Sermon on the Mount by telling His listeners to love and pray for their enemies (Matt. 5:43–48). In other words, leave vengeance and judgment to God.

If we try to do God's work, we will fail. God vindicates His people in due time. We must have patience and let God's work go forward according to His plan.

Even the Lord Jesus Christ, when He was on this earth, had to turn any thoughts of retaliation or "getting even" over to God. This is how Peter described it: "Who, when He was reviled, did not revile in return; when He suffered, He did not threaten, but committed Himself to Him who judges righteously" (1 Pet. 2:23).

LEARN TO PLAN AHEAD

After making it clear what we should not do, Paul told us what we should do: "Have regard for good things in the sight of all men" (Rom. 12:17).

The Greek word translated *regard* in this verse means to "plan ahead."[10] In other words, when you can see ahead to what's facing you, make plans to do what's right, knowing that temptation and difficulties will come. Each week pray and strategize ways to overcome the evil you face. Paul expounded on this concept further in his letter to the Thessalonians: "See that no one renders evil for evil to anyone, but always pursue what is good both for yourselves and for all" (1 Thess. 5:15).

When it comes to how we handle evil in our lives, most of us are *reactive*. But Paul is calling upon us to be *proactive*. To plan ahead, to pursue what is good instead of just reacting to what's bad.

No one is immune to the daily irritations in life. Some situations and people just naturally bring out the worst in us, don't they? Maybe it's the uncle who always talks and never listens, or an in-law who loves to ruffle your feathers with their political views. Maybe you can't stand the wait that follows, "Your call is very important to us. Please hold and a representative will be with you shortly." Or maybe your blood boils as you dodge lane-weavers on the freeway.

We're often at our worst when dealing with such people and situations. In frustration, we blurt out, "They do this to me every time!" or "She really gets under my skin!" or "He makes me so mad!"

Let me say first that no person, event, or thing can *make* you get upset or frustrated. You are responsible for your reactions to difficult people and difficult situations. That said, people and situations like this aren't going to go away, so Paul challenges us to strategize how we can do good even in unpleasant circumstances. Our task is to learn how we can do better the next time we face similar events and people.

LEAN INTO THE NEXT RIGHT THING

Whether we've planned for them or not, times of trial will come. And when they do, we must decide how to respond.

For the Christian, no response is not an option. Clearly, we cannot ignore, accept, or be passive in the face of evil. In Ephesians 6 Paul made it clear we're to take action against evil by standing—an active verb. We're to equip ourselves with the armor of God to *stand* against evil so we can overcome it.

It's also clear that we're not to seek vengeance. But what, then, are we supposed to do?

One of the best, and shortest, philosophies for living I know of is this: "Do the next right thing."

I opened this chapter with the story of a woman of remarkable courage who spoke up against abuse. When others with more power and influence ignored and covered up evil, she stepped forward and called it out. How did she find the strength to do that?

She found it through her deep faith. Rachael Denhollander compared the "good things in the sight of all men" that Paul referred to (Rom. 12:17)—what she called the "straight line" in her statement—to the "crooked line" of evil. What was being done was contrary to what she knew to be right and good, so she did the next right thing. She took a stand.

Evil can be difficult to expose. In fact, the enemy often makes it that way. We may not be able to fully explain what's occurring, or define exactly what we need. But while our spiritual armor gives us resilience and strength to stand against the obvious enemies, it also gives us what we need to stand against the confusing and subtle enemies—such as the person we trusted who betrays us, or the deliberate inaction of others in the face of evil.

As an Overcomer, we must put our trust in Christ. When in doubt, ask Him for help. Ask Him, through the Holy Spirit, to show you how to do "the next right (good) thing." Trust God that doing one right thing—one good thing after another—will overcome any wrong thing, any evil thing, in your path.

Sometimes you may not see the result of your overcoming acts. Sometimes God uses you in ways and plans that are bigger than you can understand or longer than you will live. God works in His time, not yours or mine. We're not called to witness the results; we're only called to overcome evil with good, to simply perform the good task set before us at the moment.

The famous Lewis and Clark expedition to map the Pacific Northwest was actually saved in 1805 when an act of goodness overcame an evil intent. Ken Burns tells the story in a documentary called *Lewis and Clark: The Journey of the Corps of Discovery.*

The expedition party spent a starved and freezing winter in Idaho's Bitterroot Mountains. They stumbled out of the mountains and into the camp of the Nez Perce, a Native American tribe, hoping to find food and warmth. Some of the Nez Perce wanted to kill the expedition members and take all their goods: rifles, ammunition, tools, and other hardware. But an aged and dying woman in the camp saved them from annihilation.

As a young girl, this woman had been captured by another Native American tribe, then sold to yet another tribe back east. She escaped, and ended up in the care of Canadians who sustained her until she could, years later, make her way back to her own Nez Perce people.

For years she told her people about the light-skinned people who "lived toward the rising sun" and took care of her. So, when the light-skinned members of the Lewis and Clark expedition arrived in their camp, she intervened: "These are the people who helped me. Do them no hurt."[11]

In this case, an act of good was separated from the evil it overcame by decades. The people in Canada who cared for a young Native American girl had no idea their act of goodness would turn away the evil intent of her tribe many years later. They didn't project into the future—they just did the next right thing.

LIVE PEACEABLY WITH ALL MEN

"If it is possible, as much as depends on you, live peaceably with all men" (Rom. 12:18).

The families of San Antonio next-door neighbors Rick and Tony were close friends, often visiting and attending events together, including family weddings and vacations. But in 2012, the friendship ended and a feud began, forcing police responses to over 140 complaints.

The rift began when Rick posted juicing recipes on Facebook. Tony's family claimed the concoction made them sick. Rick's wife posted a response saying if they didn't eat so much fatty foods, maybe they wouldn't be so overweight. Things went swiftly downhill from there.

A dispute over backyard trees spurred Rick to build a monstrous, twelve-foot corrugated metal wall between the two houses. Then, Tony used a cattle prod to knock down garbage cans to create nighttime noise. Rick responded by painting pigs on Tony's side of the fence and displaying toy pigs in obscene poses. Next, Tony then erected a thirteen-foot pole topped with a camera aimed over Rick's fence. Rick countered with surveillance equipment aimed at Tony's home. Tony claimed every time his family walked out of their house, Rick made pig noises and even posted videos of Tony's wife on YouTube with pig grunts dubbed in.

An altercation involving a trash can resulted in a conviction, a fine, and community service for Rick. But that wasn't enough for Tony's family. His wife put up a sign saying Rick's family were perverts. Despite police orders to remove the sign, she kept putting it back. Both families filed lawsuits and received court orders to stop everything until the suits were resolved.[12]

Can you imagine? Unfortunately, you probably can.

I am deeply concerned that this story reflects a rapidly accelerating trend toward angry conflict across our nation. Political rivalry has become political animosity; opponents spit hatred and vitriol at each other like vicious animals. It's spilled over into entertainment, where sitcoms, comedians, and even broadcasters insult, slander, and belittle those who don't share their views. In our schools, words of hate are heard where they were never tolerated before. At universities, disfavored lecturers are shouted off the stage. This behavior is exactly the opposite of what the New Testament commands:

- "Blessed are the peacemakers, for they shall be called sons of God" (Matt. 5:9).
- "Pursue peace with all people, and holiness, without which no one will see the Lord" (Heb. 12:14).

Responding to one evil act with another merely escalates the evil, as the Rick-and-Tony feud vividly demonstrates. It's like spraying gasoline on a raging fire. But when we overcome evil with good, the evil is smothered, lacking the fuel of animosity to keep it alive.

Of course, we don't have total control in these situations. When we have done *everything* in *our* power to establish and maintain peace, and yet the other person is not willing to have peace, then God does not hold us accountable for the lack of peace. But first, we must do everything within our power—and the power of Christ living in us—to live at peace with others.[13]

LET GOOD OVERCOME EVIL

A brash, hardened young defendant appeared before Judge Albert Tomei in the New York State Supreme Court. The defendant had gunned down another person, execution style. After a two-week trial resulting in a guilty verdict, the victim's mother and grandmother spoke during the sentencing phase. Both women forgave the defendant. The grandmother offered to write to him in prison if he would write to her, confessing that she'd tried to hate the young man without success. She spoke only of compassion and forgiveness.

Throughout the trial, the defendant had maintained an angry demeanor toward the judge and jury. But as the grandmother spoke to him, his body language began to change. Judge Tomei wrote:

For the first time since the trial began, the defendant's eyes lost their laser force and appeared to surrender to a life force that only a mother can generate: nurturing, unconditional love. After the grandmother finished, I looked at the defendant. His head was hanging low. There was no more swagger, no more stare. The destructive and evil forces within him collapsed helplessly before this remarkable display of humaneness.[14]

The mother and grandmother did what Paul recommended: "'If your enemy is hungry, feed him; if he is thirsty, give him a drink; for in so doing you will heap coals of fire on his head.' Do not be overcome by evil, but overcome evil with good" (Rom. 12:20–21).

Here's some of the best advice I ever received about responding to evil: when someone strikes out at you to hurt you with an evil act or accusation, don't curse it; don't rehearse it; don't nurse it—but do reverse it.

Jesus talked about reversing the impact of evil: "You have heard that it was said, 'An eye for an eye and a tooth for a tooth.' But I tell you not to resist an evil person. But whoever slaps you on your right cheek, turn the other to him also. If anyone wants to sue you and take away your tunic, let him have your cloak also" (Matt. 5:38–40).

And Peter wrote, "Not returning evil for evil or reviling for reviling, but on the contrary blessing, knowing that you were called to this, that you may inherit a blessing" (1 Pet. 3:9).

Counselor Jay Adams says that "evil is powerful, but good is more powerful. In fact, evil is so powerful that only good has the power to overcome evil. Darkness can be driven away only by light."[15]

LOVE YOUR ENEMY

The phrase Paul used in Romans 12:20—"you will heap coals of fire on his head"—is an odd one to us. He said that's what happens when we offer our enemy food and drink; that is, when we repay him with good for any evil he's done to us.

Pastor John MacArthur explains:

The phrase heap burning coals upon his head referred to an ancient Egyptian custom. When a person wanted to demonstrate public contrition, he would carry on his head a pan of burning coals to represent the burning pain of his shame and guilt. The point here is that, when we love our enemy and genuinely seek to meet his needs, we shame him for his hatred.[16]

Consider the story of David and King Saul. David was the anointed successor of King Saul, and was therefore hated and hunted by the king. On one occasion, David got so close to Saul in a dark cave that he cut off a corner of the king's robe, but he refused to harm the king in any way.

Here are David's words after he and Saul had come out of the cave:

Look, this day your eyes have seen that the LORD delivered you today into my hand in the cave, and someone urged me to kill you. But my eye spared you, and I said, "I will not stretch out my hand against my lord, for he is the LORD's anointed." Moreover, my father, see! Yes, see the corner of your robe in my hand! For in that I cut off the corner of your robe, and did not kill you, know and see that there is neither evil nor rebellion in my hand, and I have not sinned against you. Yet you hunt my life to take it. Let the LORD judge between you and me, and let the LORD avenge me on you. But my hand shall not be against you. (1 Sam. 24:10–12)

David had just heaped coals of fire on Saul's head. And what was Saul's response to this?

So it was, when David had finished speaking these words to Saul, that Saul said, "Is this your voice, my son David?" And Saul lifted up his voice and wept. Then he said to David: "You are more righteous than I; for you have rewarded me with good, whereas I have rewarded you with evil. And you have shown this day how you have dealt well with me; for when the LORD delivered me into your hand, you did not kill me. For if a man finds his enemy, will he let him get away safely? Therefore may the LORD reward you with good for what you have done to me this day." (vv. 16–19)

Someone has wisely said, "The enemy has overcome us when he makes us like himself." To repay evil for evil is to become like Satan. To adopt the methods of your enemy is to become an enemy yourself.

But to repay good for evil is to become like God.

The essential victory over evil is the work of love. Jesus said, "Love your enemies, bless those who curse you, do good to those who hate you, and pray for those who spitefully use you and persecute you" (Matt. 5:44).

Love. Bless. Do good. Pray. That is how you overcome evil with good.

This is no imaginary victory. It's the most revolutionary force in the world. Imagine what our world would be like if we employed this force every day.

Here is the essence of this lesson in one statement: Overcome evil with good. That is the Christian way. It is unique in a world of vengeance and retaliation.

KEEP ON DOING GOOD

The week before I began writing this chapter on overcoming evil with good I was in Nashville, Tennessee. When I entered the hotel elevator, an elderly, distinguished-looking African-American gentleman and his daughter got on the elevator with me. When we exchanged greetings, he asked if I was David Jeremiah; he told me he and his wife watch our *Turning Point* television show every Sunday. When I asked his name, I was shocked to discover I was speaking with John Perkins. Many times I have referenced this man's incredible story in sermons from my pulpit; he is one of the greatest Overcomers in our nation's history.

John Perkins was born in Mississippi in 1930, the child of poor sharecroppers. His mother died of complications arising from starvation when he was an infant, and his father abandoned the family. Raised by his extended family, John was seventeen when his older brother, a decorated World War II veteran, was fatally shot by a policeman and died in his arms. Filled with grief and rage, John left Mississippi for California, where he married, had children, and became a Christian.

In 1960, John felt the Lord calling him to return to racially torn Mississippi to preach the gospel. So he moved his family to Mendenhall, Mississippi, a neighboring town to the one he was raised in. There he established the Voice of Calvary Bible Institute.

In February 1970, Perkins and two associates went to the local jail to post bail for a group of black college students. He and his associates were surrounded by police officers and arrested, and Perkins was severely beaten and tortured simply for being a black leader in the community. The students and his associates feared Perkins might die as he lay unconscious on the floor of the jail cell.

Somehow, through his own pain, John Perkins realized the white people in his community needed the gospel as much as those in the black community. He understood that the law enforcement officers' hatred of him was based on prejudice and ignorance, and that acts of racism and hatred were all these angry men knew. Perkins vowed that if God would deliver him out of that situation, he would keep doing good by preaching a gospel that would heal the *whole* community.

Two local doctors—one white, one black—oversaw the healing of his physical wounds. At the same time, God healed his soul, revealing more and more about how the gospel was the only thing that freed people from evil and hatred, regardless of their skin color. John realized that Christ had suffered unjustly at the hands of hateful people, yet He still prayed that God would forgive them. In time, God gave John Perkins the ability to forgive his attackers and truly love them, and he committed himself to overcoming the terrible evil done to him with good.

John Perkins became a champion for healing broken communities, first in Mississippi and then across the nation, through the goodness of the gospel. He has received fourteen honorary doctoral degrees and written nearly a dozen books extolling the power of God's love to overcome evil with good. As I write this, John Perkins is eighty-eight years old and still doing good by working to bring the gospel of peace and understanding to a nation divided. He is truly an Overcomer![17]

You and I will never stop encountering evil in the world around us, and we'll never, this side of heaven, be totally free from the temptation to do evil ourselves. Within us and without us, there is only one power in the world strong enough to overcome evil. And that power is the goodness of God.

Righteousness is what the goodness of God looks like when lived out. If we're going to protect our hearts from evil, we must protect them with the righteousness of Christ. Jesus never failed to overcome evil with good in His life, and He gives us the ability to do the same as we walk by faith: "not having [our] own righteousness . . . but that which is through faith in Christ, the righteousness which is from God by faith" (Phil. 3:9).

Let us not become weary in doing good, for at the proper
time we will reap a harvest if we do not give up.
—GALATIANS 6:9, NIV

CHAPTER 5

OVERCOMING ANXIETY
WITH PEACE

When Houston energy worker Shawn Baker was laid off in 2015, she opened a new business that quickly became a "smash hit." It's a place for angry, stressed-out, or anxiety-filled people to take out their frustrations on inanimate objects. Inside the building are four rooms lined with thick plywood, all stocked with old furniture, dishes, burned-out TVs and appliances, out-of-date electronics, and even feather pillows Baker buys from junk dealers or used furniture shops. Customers get their choice of instrument—golf club, baseball bat, lead pipe, or sledge hammer. Then, after donning mandatory protective equipment, they close themselves in a room and smash everything in sight.

Baker named her business Tantrums, LLC.

Customers pay $25 to $50 for five to fifteen minutes of demolition. After a session, the room looks like a war zone, filled with broken glass, feathers, ceramic shards, and electronic innards. People from all walks of life flock to Baker's business—mothers, businessmen, doctors, teachers, oil and gas workers, and even some therapists.

Customers rave about how beneficial a session of smashing has been, enabling them to relieve stress in a controlled environment. Baker said, "I would have never thought I would be helping people like that."[1]

It's easy to understand the impulse that drives customers to Shawn Baker's business. Anxiety is one of the defining symptoms of our times. According to the Anxiety and Depression Association of America, anxiety disorders affect forty million adults in the United States, or just over 18 percent of the population. It's a major factor affecting our general health; people with anxiety disorders go to doctors three to five times more than the general population.[2]

Some anxiety disorders are clinical in origin, springing from genetics, brain chemistry, or both; others are the result of life events and conditions. Whatever their cause, we know rates are rising among all ages, including children and teens.

Younger and younger children are being diagnosed with anxiety, while colleges say rates of anxiety are higher than ever among their students.[3] It's not hard to see why—our world measures, grades, and judges everything young people do. Every social media post is "liked" or not, cyber-bullying is on the rise, and kids feel pressure to achieve like never before.

Seeing the anxiety of those we love can increase our own levels of worry. Dealing with the normal stress of home, work, and life is already a challenge, but at some point we'll face other pressures too: money worries, job stress, family conflict, traumatic events, addiction, caring for a loved one. Layered over these immediate concerns is the general sense that our world, our country, and our communities are increasingly unsafe, plagued by international conflict, political discord, rising anger and incivility, violence, and even climate uncertainty.

When it comes to dealing with these fears and stresses, most of us realize that smashing a microwave in a safe room is not going to cut it. Behind this kind of therapy is the idea that our fears and frustrations build tension that can only be released through violence. Certainly, taking a sledge hammer to a TV set is better than taking our emotions out on others, but the theory that anxiety can be banished and peace achieved through the application of violence is simply not true.

In His wisdom, God has provided support for those who need it through medication, counseling, and support groups. I urge you to seek help whenever you or your loved ones need it. A life in Christ does not remove us from the world; it sustains us in it. Thankfully, one of the ways Christ sustains us in this world is through the gift of peace.

THE SHOES OF PEACE

The third implement of warfare on the Ephesians 6 list is put there to help you overcome anxiety. Here's how Paul described that piece of armor: "Stand therefore . . . having shod your feet with the preparation of the gospel of peace" (vv. 14–15). The New Living Translation renders this verse: "For shoes, put on the peace that comes from the Good News so that you will be fully prepared."

The shoes Paul used for his illustration were not the average person's shoes; they were the open-toed leather boots worn by Roman soldiers. Made with nail-studded soles designed to grip the ground, they resembled our modern cleated football shoes. These boots were not made for running or even for marching. Instead, they were specifically designed for one primary purpose: to give the soldier stability in hand-to-hand combat against the enemy.[4]

The Christians of that day would have understood what this meant: in hand-to-hand combat, the first to accidentally lose his footing is the first to fall!

Battling anxiety is like fighting the enemy in close combat in your mind. If you're unprepared, Satan sees that vulnerability. If you feel doubt, fear, hesitation, or uncertainty, he sees those things too. And whatever Satan observes, he uses to his advantage.

If you struggle with anxiety of any kind, you know that worry can surface many times a day. Maybe it's a chronic, nagging voice telling you that you're not good enough and never will be. Maybe it's the aftermath of fear and trauma from violence or loss. Perhaps you struggle with a fear of rejection that makes you blurt out hurtful words before you can be hurt. Or maybe you exhaust yourself trying to control every aspect of your and your family's lives in a vain effort to ease the constant worry and anxiety that hover at the edges of your mind.

But what would happen if instead of fear and vulnerability, the enemy saw preparation and strength in you? What if he saw certainty, faith, and trust? What if he saw that you, dealing with tough challenges and your own human limitations, were also standing strong in the peace of Christ?

Then the enemy would be facing an Overcomer! And that is what God has designed you to be. Not perfect, not invulnerable, not unaffected by life. But strong, resolute, and successful in your path, able to overcome worry with the peace of Christ.

Just as the Roman soldier's studded shoes anchored him firmly to the ground as he faced his opponent, peace anchors us firmly to God as we face the troubles and uncertainties that assail us in this fallen world.

PEACE THROUGH CHRIST

The Bible teaches that life apart from Christ has no deep peace. Everyone is aware of this cosmic discomfort to some degree. As British novelist Julian Barnes quipped, "I don't believe in God, but I miss Him."[5]

This emptiness has been evident throughout history, even in ancient times when primitive cultures, sensing alienation from the powers above, lived in fear and cringing, believing that storms, earthquakes, and floods were manifestations of divine disapproval.

Many of us today have a similar acute awareness that our lives are not right. But when we come to Jesus Christ and put our trust in Him, the Bible says this about us: "Therefore, having been justified by faith, we have peace with God through our Lord Jesus Christ" (Rom. 5:1).

The peace that Jesus is giving to us here is a peace that was purchased at the price of His own blood. It is our legacy because of the cross. He has bequeathed it to all of us. We're responsible for living in the light of the great provision God has given us in Jesus Christ as our peace. When we do, we know that in Christ there is no condemnation.

After the birth of Lindsey Carlson's fifth baby, she began to have full-blown panic attacks. Like one in eight mothers, Lindsey was suffering from postpartum depression, the number one complication of childbirth. Although she'd struggled after the birth of her fourth child, this time was very different.

"This dark valley was more physically painful and threatening than any I'd previously experienced," Lindsey shared. "I felt like an empty shell of a person. I knew I wasn't myself, but no matter how much I prayed, read Scripture, or tried to get better, I couldn't snap out of it."[6]

As common as it is, postpartum depression (PPD) often goes undiagnosed, partly because symptoms can vary. But according to the *American Journal of Clinical Medicine*, there's also another reason: "The majority of undiagnosed cases are probably due to the social stigma of being labeled an 'unhappy mother,' not to mention the public image of PPD."[7]

Sadly, as Lindsey notes, Christian moms can face an *additional* barrier to seeking help.

For those who love Jesus and want to glorify him, it's embarrassing to admit feeling overwhelmed by the children God gave us. . . .

It's easy to worry that admitting any struggles may be perceived as sinful, faithless, or reflect a lack of gratitude for what God's given. Inside the church, women who suffer with PPD [postpartum depression] may actually receive correction instead of grace and judgment instead of hope.

Fortunately, Lindsey had the courage to apply the gospel to her condition, and she sought and received medical help.

[Jesus] knows the Enemy's temptations, he knows the feeling of being pushed past physical limits, and he knows the longing for freedom from pain. . . . When we are feeling our lowest and questioning our faith or God's willingness to deliver us from the pain of PPD, we must remember the gospel: the good news that Jesus saves. . . .

Our standing with God and his acceptance of us is not based on our ability to be a good mom, to trust God enough to overcome PPD, or on how we feel. . . . PPD cannot separate us from God. Paul encourages believers by assuring them, "There is now no condemnation for those who are in Christ Jesus" (Rom. 8:1). Because Christ suffered and died for you, you are freed from the shame of postpartum depression.[8]

If you struggle with anxiety, life can seem like a battle. But God understands the extent of your worry. And because of the gospel of peace, the one thing you don't have to fear is losing His love. Even in the darkest nights of the soul, the God of all peace is *with* you and *for* you.

I urge you to embrace these words of the apostle Peter: "Humble yourselves, therefore, under God's mighty hand, that he may lift you up in due time. Cast all your anxiety on him because he cares for you" (1 Pet. 5:6–7, NIV).

A PEACE BEYOND UNDERSTANDING

On more than one occasion, Jesus told His disciples there is a peace that is available to them at all times—one that is capable of calming their hearts in any storm in life.

- "Peace I leave with you, My peace I give to you; not as the world gives do I give to you. Let not your heart be troubled, neither let it be afraid" (John 14:27).
- "These things I have spoken to you, that in Me you may have peace. In the world you will have tribulation; but be of good cheer, I have overcome the world" (John 16:33).

Jesus spoke these words to His disciples when He knew that in a matter of hours their lives would be shattered through His own terrible ordeal and death. And yet He told them they could have peace in the midst of trauma—an inward peace that brings confidence and stability.

The peace Jesus gives us is not a promise to remove the pain and stress of daily living. Those troubles are inevitable, and they will not be removed from us until the Lord comes again. The peace He offers is a calm, unafraid, unruffled confidence that, having placed our lives in His hands, all will be well. Nothing can harm our innermost being. Nothing can shake us from the intimate connection we've established with the Lord of the universe through our saving faith in Him. It's a peace we have despite external circumstances—a peace that cannot be destroyed.

Eric Barker was a Christian missionary who spent fifty years preaching the gospel in Portugal in the years leading up to World War II and beyond. What was a challenging mission field in the best of times became even more stressful as the war gained momentum. At some point things became so dangerous in Portugal that he was advised to send his wife and eight children by boat to England, as well as his sister and her three children. So he loaded the thirteen people he treasured most in the world onto a ship and watched it steam out of sight. His plan was to join his family in England on a later ship after concluding some missionary business in Portugal.

The Sunday after his family's departure was a Sunday like most— except for a telegram he received shortly before the service began, a telegram he shared with his congregation: "I've just received word that all my family have arrived safely home." The congregation breathed a sigh of relief and the service continued.

It was only later that the full meaning of the pastor's words became known to the congregation: "Safely home" didn't mean "safely in England." Just before the meeting, Barker learned that a German U-boat had torpedoed the ship carrying his family; there were no survivors. His wife, their eight children, and his sister and her three children were all lost. But Barker knew exactly where they were. They were indeed "safely home" with the Lord.[9]

Even as I share this story, it seems beyond imagination. Yet in my years of pastoring, I've witnessed remarkable examples of the peace that is possible in the face of extreme tragedy and grief. I've seen many believers manifest this peace of God as they walked through the deep shadow cast by the death of a child or as they struggled with a debilitating disease. The world looks at people bearing such heavy burdens and wonders how they do it. No wonder Paul called this a peace that "surpasses all understanding" (Phil. 4:7).

EXPERIENCING GOD'S PEACE

Is it possible to find peace when facing danger? The answer is yes. During the darkest times, when anxiety wants to overwhelm you, the answer is still yes. Even if you are facing death itself.

Dietrich Bonhoeffer was a young German pastor and theologian imprisoned in Nazi Germany for his resistance to Hitler and the Third Reich. During two years of imprisonment, he ministered to his fellow prisoners and wrote many letters to family and friends on the outside. His letters were smuggled out of prison by sympathetic German guards and later published posthumously as *Letters and Papers from Prison*. They reveal a man living in peace, sustained by prayer, devoted to Scripture, and confident of the new life that awaited him should he die.

After Bonhoeffer was hanged in April 1945, an English military officer imprisoned with the pastor wrote of him, "Bonhoeffer . . . was all humility and sweetness, he always seemed to diffuse an atmosphere of happiness, of joy in every smallest event in life, and of deep gratitude for the mere fact that he was alive. . . . He was one of the very few men that I have ever met to whom his God was real and close to him."[10]

When we have made peace with God and have the peace of God in our lives, we can hold our ground and overcome any assault by our enemy. Our faith, like those cleated shoes, will hold firm and not allow us to slip or fall. Our Lord desires this twofold peace for each of us. But the gap between those who've made peace with God by accepting Christ as their Savior and those who actually experience the peace of God—a supernatural sense of calm and confidence when life is chaotic—seems to be growing wider.

Unfortunately, I meet more and more Christians who think just because they are believers in Christ—just because they read the Bible, just because they have the Holy Spirit living in them, just because "all things have become new" (2 Cor. 5:17)—they should be immune from life's pressures. They mistakenly define peace as the removal of trouble rather than a way of living joyfully and worry-free in spite of trouble.

When the pressures of life come crashing in, many turn to money, drugs, alcohol, various means of escapism, inappropriate relationships, and other sources for relief. Some may choose to smash household goods at Tantrum, LLC. But none of these remedies lasts. When the temporary effect wears off, we're left with more anxiety than before—and for the believer, a greater sense of guilt and despair.

But God has a plan for you that will last. Two central passages in the Bible give us positive, workable strategies to address the subject of anxiety. They're found in Philippians 4 and Matthew 6. What are these strategies? We can reveal them by asking the five standard questions commonly posed by journalists: How? What? Who? Where? and When?

HOW ARE YOU PRAYING?

Do you know the most often highlighted verses in the entire Bible today? According to Amazon's Kindle tracking, they are Paul's words about anxiety:[11]

> Be anxious for nothing, but in everything by prayer and supplication, with thanksgiving, let your requests be made known to God; and the peace of God, which surpasses all understanding, will guard your hearts and minds through Christ Jesus. (Phil. 4:6–7)

In this passage, the word *anxious* literally means to be pulled in two different directions.[12] It means to have a war, a battle going on in your inner spirit that's pulling you apart inside.

Someone has said, "If it is big enough to worry about, it is big enough to pray about." Martin Luther wrote, "Pray, and let God worry."[13] And Mark Batterson encourages us to "think of worry as a prayer alarm. Every time it goes off, you put it to prayer."[14]

So my first question is this: How are you praying? (I won't ask *if* you're praying, because if you're facing anxiety in your life—you pray!) And I'm not talking about the words you say or whether you kneel, sit, or clasp hands. I'm asking what kind of prayer you pray. When I'm facing stress and turbulence in my life, two kinds of prayers are helpful: progressive prayer and proactive prayer.

PROGRESSIVE PRAYER

When we're under pressure, our tendency is to rush into His presence with our list of needs without even saying "Hello" to the Lord: "God, I need this, this, this, this, and this. And I need it now, and tomorrow, and the next day. If You could go ahead and get it done ahead of time, that would be even better."

Sound familiar? Real prayer is a lifestyle of love for the Lord. Rushing into His presence with our laundry list of needs without pausing to truly focus on Him can depress us more than if we hadn't prayed at all! Have you ever started talking to God about your problems and found yourself more overwhelmed than when you started? It's because you're focusing on your problems instead of focusing on God!

A long time ago, someone gave me a four-step outline for prayer that forms an acrostic spelling of the word *ACTS*: Adoration, Confession, Thanksgiving, Supplication. I recommend it to you as a simple way to order your prayers.

- *Adoration:* Set your prayer list aside as soon as you enter God's presence. Spend some time simply worshiping Him for who He is. Recognizing and acknowledging God's greatness allows your needs and problems to be seen in proper perspective.
- *Confession:* Tell your sins to God. Repent, or turn away from them in your heart, and ask sincerely for His forgiveness. Knowing Jesus died for you and intercedes for you with His Father, let God's forgiveness wash over your spirit.
- *Thanksgiving:* Express your gratitude to God. This is a joyous exercise! Thank Him for His love and mercy and for

the blessings in your life. When you linger in gratitude and thanksgiving, your heart is healed and your spirit uplifted.

- *Supplication:* Humbly ask God for what you need. Be specific, trusting Him to take care of your problems and replace them with joy. Ask the Holy Spirit to enter your life and grow you in faith, love, and hope. Close your prayer in peace.

By building our prayer on these four progressive elements, we come into God's presence and experience a deeper fellowship with Him. We adore Him with praise, confess our sins, thank Him for His blessings, and present our supplications (requests) to Him. Following that simple outline will go a long way toward helping you overcome the anxiety in your life.

Remember, an improper perspective distorts reality. Hold a dime-sized pebble an inch from your eye and it will block the view of the most majestic mountain. But take the pebble away and you'll see the mountain and the pebble in their proper relationship to each other.

That's how it is with prayer. Your anxieties, held too close, can blind you to the truth of God's majesty. When you focus on His majesty, you come away with your perspective restored.

PROACTIVE PRAYER

Here's something I've learned about prayer that I've never seen mentioned in any book on prayer: prayer is meant to be both preventative and proactive. We usually treat prayer as remedial, meaning we pray when we have a need or find ourselves in trouble. But in Luke 18:1, Jesus says that we "always ought to pray and not lose heart."

Proactive prayer is learning to pray in advance of hardship, asking for the strength to face challenges before they hit us. By praying in advance to overcome anxiety, you're preparing for the inevitable when your mind is clear and rational. Praying this way draws the power of the Holy Spirit into the picture, giving you future strength to overcome difficulty.

In other words, prayer shouldn't be your last thought; it should be your first thought—before you're overcome with doubt and fear. Before you're vulnerable.

When it comes to temptation, here's how Jesus instructed us to pray: "And do not lead us into temptation, but deliver us from the evil one" (Matt. 6:13). In other words, Jesus is telling us to pray first, all the time, even when we're strong, so that we may not enter into temptation. Stress and difficulty will come. Fear will creep into our thinking and worry will become our normal state—unless we constantly affirm our strength in the peace of Christ by asking Him to bring that peace upon us.

Hugh Cairns was lord chancellor of the United Kingdom in 1868 and 1874–1880. Each day in office his schedule was packed with meetings and countless decisions to make. Lord Cairns reportedly said "that if he had accomplished anything in the world, he attributed it to the fact that the first two hours of every day of his life for years had been given to communion with God in secret prayer and the study of His Word." Cairns said, "Do you suppose I come to a Cabinet meeting without first having talked it over with God?"[15]

Prayer was not a last resort for Cairns. It was his first resort—praying before the crisis even arose. When you're not anxious, stressed, or under pressure, that's when you thank God for His strength, and that's when you pray to be shored up and defended against the pressures that will surely come.

WHAT ARE YOU THINKING?

In Philippians 4, Paul wrote, "Whatever things are true, whatever things are noble, whatever things are just, whatever things are pure, whatever things are lovely, whatever things are of good report, if there is any virtue and if there is anything praiseworthy—meditate on these things" (v. 8).

With this list, Paul is telling us exactly and specifically what we are to think on, making it clear that we can and should direct our thoughts to what he describes. This is a command, an action statement. It is what we are to employ our minds in doing.

Our thought life is to be positive, uplifting, and redemptive because our thought life is the launching pad for our active, outward life. If you want your mind to be free of anxiety, make determined, definite choices as to what you allow into it. I cannot stress this enough. You are the guardian of your mind.

Max Lucado explains:

> You probably know this, but in case you don't, I am so thrilled to give you the good news: you can pick what you ponder.
>
> You didn't select your birthplace or birth date. You didn't choose your parents or siblings. You don't determine the weather or the amount of salt in the ocean. There are many things in life over which you have no choice. But the greatest activity of life is well within your dominion. You can choose what you think about. You can be the air traffic controller of your mental airport. You occupy the control tower and can direct the mental traffic of your world. Thoughts circle above, coming and going. If one of them lands, it is because you gave it permission. If it leaves, it is because you directed it to do so. You can select your thought pattern. . . .
>
> It turns out that our most valuable weapon against anxiety weighs less than three pounds and sits between our ears. Think about what you think about![16]

God wants our minds to be so saturated with His truth that we learn to see life from His perspective. He is certainly at peace, and when we see Him as He is, we can be at peace as well. Learn to rest your thoughts on the Almighty. When troubles arise, direct your thoughts to the Father's love and care for you in all things; trust in His wisdom.

The story is told of a man who was on a long-haul flight when the voice of the captain came across the speakers. "Ladies and gentlemen, please fasten your seat belts. I'm asking the flight attendants to be seated and we're suspending beverage service because we're expecting turbulence ahead."

Turbulence is what they got. Within minutes, the plane was trembling, then quaking from the storm. Cracks of thunder could be heard above the roar of the engines. Lightning lit up the darkening skies, and the plane jolted like a cork tossed around on a heavenly ocean. One moment the airplane was lifted on terrific currents of air; the next it dropped as if about to crash. The man was as terrified as the other passengers. Only one person seemed perfectly calm: a little girl, her feet tucked beneath her as she curled up reading a book amid the mayhem. Sometimes she closed her eyes as if napping.

Gradually the plane escaped the storm and finally flew peacefully on to its destination. While waiting to disembark, the man couldn't help asking the girl why she had not worried. "My daddy's the pilot," she said, "and he's taking me home. I didn't worry because I knew he was in the cockpit."[17]

In the midst of the storm, we need to set our minds on the One who is at the controls—almighty God. We can rest secure in Him as He takes us home.

Isaiah 26:3 is a prayer for us to echo: "You will keep him in perfect peace, whose mind is stayed on You, because he trusts in You."

WHO ARE YOU FOLLOWING?

To overcome anxiety, you can't just think about what is good, right, and true. You must also begin living it out. Often that means having a mentor who can show you the way. That's why Paul wrote to the Philippian church, "The things which you learned and received and heard and saw in me, these do, and the God of peace will be with you" (Phil. 4:9).

Paul's message to the Philippian believers was this: take the lessons I've taught you and practice the things you've seen me do, and you, too, will begin to experience the presence of the God of peace.

If you battle anxiety, surround yourself with others who've learned how to trust the Lord when life is overwhelming. Spend time with people who understand the complexities of anxiety and the keys to success. Ask them questions. Study their lives. Listen to their stories. Learn from them.

Perhaps it's time to make an appointment with a doctor or wise counselor, ask a friend to meet you for coffee, join a small group at church, or simply pick up and read an encouraging book about someone—maybe even the apostle Paul—who learned how to hand their anxious cares over to the Lord.

Let God's peace in their lives influence the anxiety in yours.

When anxiety hit him "like a full-blown tornado," pastor and author Tommy Nelson learned that extreme stress over long periods of time can impact the physical body and those physical responses can then impact the mind. After his first panic attack, which sent him to the doctor fearing a heart attack, he realized he'd been experiencing signs of anxiety for two years.

Eventually, Nelson stepped away from his church to heal. He eliminated the initial cause of his anxiety, chronic overwork and stress, but a terrible physiological damage had been done to his system.

> It is terrifying when your mind—your very means of perception— becomes impaired. . . . My greatest joy in life was my Bible, yet I could not read it for over thirty seconds. . . . Natural sleep was now impossible. For four months, I did not fall asleep without help from medication.

I was the man who had just finished addressing an association of Christian counselors. I had written books on marriage and success in life. I had written an entire overview of the Bible, and yet here I was needing someone to counsel me. . . . It was the lowest point in my life.[18]

Even though a doctor diagnosed his condition as anxiety and depression, Nelson could not bring himself to act on that advice.

At this point, I realized the great dilemma a Christian with this problem faces. Try as you may to quote Bible verses on anxiousness, your body simply will not respond. You may as well tell a quadriplegic to work through the numbness and walk. . . .

I just continued day after day as Marley's ghost. I could not go forward and reclaim my life, but I was not about to go to a hospital either.[19]

And that's when, lost in the darkness of depression, he followed wiser and stronger people, people who had his best interest at heart, and some who'd walked the path he now trod. That's also when those people stepped up to be his guides.

People going through depression usually have a safe person or safe place where the depression feels lighter. My wife was my safe person. Sometimes Teresa would go to shop for groceries, and I would follow along with her like a handicapped child—which is what I was.[20]

Others came forward to support him too.

A fellow in my church named Carl had, years earlier, been through all I was now experiencing. When he came to me, he told me everything I was feeling, because he had been there. I would say to him, "Tell me I'm going to make it through this." Carl always answered, "You're gonna make it—I promise you."[21]

Finally, after talking to Nelson's wife, a caring friend put the family in touch with another doctor. That doctor's matter-of-fact expertise opened Nelson's eyes, and he started the medication that eventually brought him out of the darkness.

As we seek to walk away from anxiety, sometimes our path is to lead the way through the darkness alone. Sometimes it is to follow a trusted advisor until we see the light again.

WHERE ARE YOU LIVING?

We've seen the "how," "what," and "who." Now it's time to examine the "where" of finding peace. Where do your thoughts reside? Where are you living? There are only three possible answers: the past, the future, or the present.

Jesus said, "Therefore do not worry about tomorrow, for tomorrow will worry about its own things. Sufficient for the day is its own trouble" (Matt. 6:34).

Think about it. The past exists only as mere memory, and the future exists only in the imagination. Only the present exists as true reality. So why do we ruin the only moment of existence we have by pulling trouble from nonexistent places?

On July 27, 2013, Rick Warren—founding pastor of Saddleback Church and author of *The Purpose Driven Life*—returned to his pulpit for the first time in four months. For 112 days, one day at a time, Pastor Warren had been seeking the Lord after his youngest son took his own life at age twenty-seven.

When Pastor Warren returned to his pulpit that Sunday in July, he began a new series of messages titled "How to Get Through What You're Going Through." And here is the first point in that first sermon: "Life doesn't make sense, but we can have peace because we know God is with us and loves us."[22]

That's what you learn after losing your son to suicide and spending one day at a time with God for four months: *we can have peace because of God's presence and His love.*

Three years later, having worked diligently through his and his family's grief and recovery, Pastor Warren published an article on his personal website titled "Trust One Day at a Time." Based on Philippians 4:6–8, he began by writing, "God wants you to trust him one day at a time: 'Give us this day our daily bread.' Not for next week. Not for next year. Not for next month. Just one day at a time." And he then wrote the same four steps I've highlighted in this chapter from Philippians 4: worry about nothing, pray about everything, thank God in all things, and think about the right things.[23]

That's how you have peace every day. You trust God and receive His peace one day at a time. You won't sink under the burden if you limit yourself to taking on today's problems. But taking on tomorrow's agenda today puts you over the weight limit.

In *Slaying the Giants in Your Life*, I wrote these words:

> There is a reason God placed us within the moment, bracketed away from both the past and the future. They are both off-limits to us, and we need to post "No Trespassing" signs. The past is closed for good, and the future is still under construction. But today has everything you need. Come here and make your home.[24]

Anxiety about the future makes you more anxious in the present. But Jesus told us not to dwell on our tomorrows. He was echoing the truth of Deuteronomy 33:25: "As your days, so shall your strength be."

WHEN WILL YOU FIND PEACE?

Perhaps you remember the graphic photo of the "Napalm Girl" from the Vietnam War. It's a painful picture to see—a naked nine-year-old running down a dirty street, arms flapping, face twisted in horror. Other children are running with her, and behind them are billowing clouds of napalm wafting toward them and burning their skin.

The girl's name is Kim Phuc Phan Thi, and she was caught in a South Vietnamese bombing raid of a route used by Viet Cong rebels. The photographer who took that photo, Nick Ut, put down his camera (which he had instinctively picked up) and quickly transported her to a hospital, saving her life.

Kim endured decades of physical suffering. For many years she prayed to the gods of Cao Dai, her family's traditional religion, for healing; no answers came. Kim's dream was to become a doctor, and she actually began studies in that field. But the world knew her in a different way, and her government forced her to leave school to be available to speak and tour.

Devastated and desperate, seeking answers, she went to Saigon's central library and started pulling Vietnamese books of religion off the shelves, one by one. The stack in front of her contained a New Testament. After thumbing through several books, she opened the New Testament and began to read in the Gospels. She was gripped by the sufferings of Christ as He bore our sins on the cross.

Shortly afterward, on Christmas Eve, 1982, Kim gave her life to Christ at a worship service. The message that day was about the Prince of Peace, Jesus Christ. Kim wrote:

How desperately I needed peace. How ready I was for love and joy. I had so much hatred in my heart—so much bitterness. I wanted to let go of all my pain. I wanted to pursue life instead of holding fast to fantasies of death. I wanted this Jesus.

So when the pastor finished speaking, I stood up, stepped out into the aisle, and made my way to the front of the sanctuary to say yes to Jesus Christ.

And there, in a small church in Vietnam, mere miles from the street where my journey had begun amid the chaos of war—on the night before the world would celebrate the birth of the Messiah—I invited Jesus into my heart.

When I woke up that Christmas morning, I experienced the kind of healing that can only come from God. I was finally at peace.[25]

Many years later, Kim married and emigrated to Canada. She reconnected with the photographer, whom she calls Uncle Nick, and they talk every week. Today Kim's life purpose is to heal others through the love and peace of Christ.

Most remarkably, Kim ultimately forgave everyone who had harmed her. She rose above her physical and emotional scars and made a choice to embrace the hope of salvation through forgiveness. She understood that unless she could forgive, she could not grow closer to Christ or bring others into His fold.

When will you find the peace of God? When you make the how, what, who, and where of His peace your priorities. Look at how you are praying, what you are thinking, who you are following, and where your thoughts are living. When you embrace these steps, then let our Lord fill your Overcomer's heart with His peace.

Now may the Lord of peace Himself give
you peace always in every way.
—2 THESSALONIANS 3:16

CHAPTER 6

OVERCOMING FEAR WITH FAITH

While he was in college, my friend Ken Davis delivered a talk to his speech class on the law of the pendulum. This law says that when a free-hanging weight swings back and forth, it will swing a shorter and shorter distance due to the effects of gravity and friction. Eventually it will stop and hang dead unless restarted.

To demonstrate, from a pivot at the top of a blackboard, Ken hung a three-foot string with a small weight attached at the bottom, creating a simple pendulum. Setting the pendulum in motion so that it swung parallel to the blackboard, he made a mark on the blackboard at each outward point where the pendulum reached in its arc. As the pendulum continued to swing, the length of each arc decreased, causing the marks to grow closer and closer to the center of the blackboard. That demonstrated the law of the pendulum in action.

"The law states that a swinging pendulum never again reaches the point from which it began its previous arc," Ken declared. "Who believes that statement is true?" A show of hands indicated he had convinced both the professor and the class.

But Ken wasn't finished. Next, he asked his professor to stand with his back against the wall. Using a much heavier weight, which he'd previously attached to the ceiling with a strong rope, he pulled the weight from its center point, held it just an inch from the professor's nose, and let it go. The weight swung away from the professor, reached the end of its arc, and started back—heading straight for the professor's face. But it never came close to touching the professor because he was gone! The sight of the weight heading straight at him was more than he could take, and he dove out of the way.[1]

The professor may have said he believed in the law of the pendulum, but he wasn't willing to put his faith to the test. Ken's point? Faith can only be proven by actions.

For followers of Jesus, a lack of faith is seldom a matter of disbelief; it's usually a matter of fear. As C. S. Lewis wrote, "Faith . . . is the art of holding on to things your reason has once accepted, in spite of your changing moods."[2] Our moods—that is, our emotions, such as fear—exert such an influence that unless mastered they can destroy our trust in what we know to be true.

We usually think of faith as a biblical or theological term. But we demonstrate faith every day in the routines of our life. Think about flying—the faith it takes to step into a metal tube and hurl through the air thirty thousand feet above the ground while going five hundred miles per hour. And the terminology defining air flight doesn't help. We end our flight at a *terminal*—a word we dread to hear from our doctors—which the flight attendant assures us we'll reach as we make our *final approach*. Then we're told to stay seated until the plane comes to a *complete* stop. (I always wonder what an *incomplete* stop would feel like.)

Who came up with this terminology? Of course, we don't help matters by choosing the airline that offers the *cheapest flights*. Yet despite all these opportunities for fear, we exercise faith continually by putting our lives in the hands of the airline industry.

Every day you act on faith in human beings. If you can put your faith in the pilot of an airplane, surely you can put your faith in Jesus.

THE SHIELD OF FAITH

Now we come to the fourth military implement the apostle Paul listed in the closing verses of Ephesians 6: "Above all, taking the shield of faith with which you will be able to quench all the fiery darts of the wicked one" (v. 16).

Paul was describing the large shield Roman infantry used to protect their whole bodies. These shields were four feet tall and two-and-a-half feet wide. Made of leather stretched over wood, they were reinforced with metal at the top and bottom.[3]

In ancient times, enemy soldiers would dip the tips of their darts or arrows into a solution of lethal poison. Even if those darts only grazed a soldier's skin, the poison would spread through his bloodstream, producing a swift and painful death. On other occasions the enemy would dip their darts in pitch and ignite them before shooting them into the Roman camp, setting it on fire.

Of all the implements of warfare included in Paul's description of the Roman soldier, this is the only piece that is given a plainly specified purpose. Paul tells us that the purpose of the shield of faith is to protect us from "all the fiery darts of the wicked one."

According to New Testament scholar Peter O'Brien, these fiery darts represent "every kind of attack launched by the devil and his hosts against the people of God. They are as wide-ranging as the 'insidious wiles' that promote them, and include not only every kind of temptation to ungodly behavior, doubt, and despair, but also external assaults, such as persecution or false teaching."[4]

If you are a Christian, then throughout your lifetime you will be bombarded by thousands of fiery arrows launched by Satan and his minions. The only way to protect yourself is through faith. The apostle John wrote, "This is the victory that has overcome the world—our faith" (1 John 5:4).

WHAT IS FAITH?

So how does faith work, and how does it overcome the fiery arrows (attacks) of the evil one? First, remember that faith involves more than mere belief. "Even the demons believe—and tremble!" (James 2:19).

As Kent Hughes tells us, in the simplest of terms, "faith . . . is belief plus trust. It is resting in the person of God and His Word to us."[5]

Faith is an active practice built on belief. Faith is not ambiguous; it's not unsure. It's a concrete conviction. It's the present-day confidence of a future reality. Faith is solid, unshakeable confidence in God built upon the assurance that He is faithful to His promises.

At age nine, Marla Runyan was diagnosed with Stargardt Disease, a degenerative macular condition that soon left her legally blind. Objects in front of Runyan appear as empty spaces. Around the periphery of her vision she can make out vague forms and colors.

Runyan was determined that her impairment would not ruin her life. After high school, she attended San Diego State, where she earned two master's degrees with the help of special equipment and volunteer readers. While there, she began competing in track events. From 1992 to 1999, she won five gold medals in the Paralympic Games, including the 1,500-meter race at the Pan American Games.

In 2000 and again in 2004, Runyan qualified for the US Olympic team and became the first legally blind person to compete in the Olympic Games, placing eighth—the top American woman finisher—in the 1,500-meter event in Sydney, Australia. In 2006, she won her second national championship in the 20K event.

Runyan learned to stay in her lane and make the turns on the track using her limited peripheral vision. Although she could not see how far she had run during a race, she learned to pace herself by hearing the intensity of her competitors' breathing. One baffled interviewer asked how she could run toward a finish line she couldn't even see. She replied, "I can't see it, but I know it's there."[6]

By faith we move forward even when the destination is not clear. Faith says that what God has promised will happen, and it's so certain that it's almost as if it has already happened. Faith treats things that are hoped for as a reality. That's the description of faith given in Hebrews 11:1: "Now faith is the substance of things hoped for, the evidence of things not seen."

Dr. Martin Luther King Jr. expressed this need for trust when he said, "Faith is taking the first step even when you don't see the whole staircase."[7]

THE JOURNEY OF FAITH

My wife, Donna, and I share a love for two verses of Scripture in the book of Proverbs: "Trust in the LORD with all your heart, and lean not on your own understanding; in all your ways acknowledge Him, and He shall direct your paths" (Prov. 3:5–6).

When I look back over my life, there have been five major occasions when this principle—this word from God—changed and deepened our walk with God. When we were seniors in college and engaged to be married, I came to believe God was calling me to be a pastor. My college education had not adequately prepared me for that role, so after listening for God's word again, I decided to go to Dallas Theological Seminary to prepare for the ministry. Then I followed God's direction to become the Christian education director and youth pastor of the Haddon Heights Baptist Church in New Jersey after graduation. Years later, God called us to Fort Wayne, Indiana, and then later to San Diego, California.

In each of those situations, I trusted God rather than my own intuition. I acted on what I believed God was telling me to do. Looking back on it from my current perspective, I can see what He was up to and how He directed our paths. But even now the hardest part of my faith journey is still the "lean not on your own understanding" part.

I suspect it's the hardest part of your faith journey too.

Trust is not easy; it's much easier to walk by sight than by faith. Walking by sight makes sense. We want to see where we're going before we set out. We rely on our physical senses, our logic, and our common sense. We set our goal, weigh the obstacles against our assets, then plan our route.

If this is the modus operandi of your Christian life, I urge you to heed my next words very carefully: if what God asks you to do always seems logical and makes sense to you, *it's probably not God you're listening to.*

As Mark Batterson has written, "Faith is not logical. But it's not illogical either. Faith is *theo*logical. . . . It just adds God into the equation."[8]

FAITH IS AMAZING

In Hebrews 11, we find an inspiring litany of some of God's most faithful people who could not see the finish line but knew it was there. The faith of these saints spurred them to action even in uncertain and fearful circumstances. They were risk-takers, mold-breakers, and system-shakers. Most of all, they were faith-walkers—and we need to be just like them!

From their lives we learn what true faith can look like. Faith brings the proper sacrifice. Faith enables one to walk with God. Faith builds an ark when it has never rained before. Faith begins a journey obediently despite not knowing the final destination. Faith dwells in tents in a foreign country. Faith looks for a city whose builder and maker is God. Faith gives a mother strength to bear a child when she is past the age of child-bearing. Faith is being willing to sacrifice one's own son in obedience. Faith believes in the resurrection. Faith promises not to leave Joseph's bones in Egypt. Faith refuses to be called the son of Pharaoh's daughter. Faith chooses to suffer affliction with the people of God. Faith esteems the reproach of Christ as greater than the treasures of Egypt.

Faith forsakes Egypt for the promised land. Faith passes through the Red Sea as on dry ground. Faith walks around Jericho until the walls fall down. Faith subdues kingdoms, works righteousness, obtains promises, stops the mouths of lions, quenches the violence of fire, escapes the edge of the sword, and turns to flight the armies of the enemy. Faith receives the dead back to life, and faith receives the promise.

Do such great deeds of faith make you feel that perhaps your own faith is small in comparison? Don't worry. Your faith can—and should—grow. Paul eagerly desired the increase of the Corinthians' faith (2 Cor. 10:15), and he wanted to visit the believers in Thessalonica to strengthen what was lacking in their faith (1 Thess. 3:10). And in his second letter to them, he commended them for the growth in their faith (2 Thess. 1:3).[9]

The New Testament recounts two times when Jesus was "amazed." Both have to do with faith. On one occasion, a Roman centurion sent messengers to Jesus to seek healing for his servant. What made this Roman's faith extraordinary was his conviction that it wasn't necessary for Jesus to travel to the servant's bedside. He knew if Jesus just said the word, the servant would be healed. Jesus "was amazed" because this Gentile, who wouldn't have been expected to have faith in Jesus at all, had astounding faith in the simple power of His word (Luke 7:1–9, NIV).

The second time Jesus was amazed by faith it was because of the lack of it. When Jesus went to His hometown of Nazareth, where faith might have been expected, "He was amazed at their unbelief" (Mark 6:6, NIV).

We can see why Jesus would have been amazed: those who should have had faith didn't, while those in whom faith was unexpected did. If we want to amaze Jesus, having faith in Him is a good place to start. If we want to live as Overcomers of our fears and failures, we must strengthen our faith and trust in the Lord.

Here are five key strategies to help you grow your faith.

TO GROW OUR FAITH, WE NEED PREACHING

Nicky Cruz was born in Puerto Rico to witchcraft-practicing parents who abused him profoundly. At fifteen, boiling with anger and rage, he was sent to New York to live with a brother. Instead, Nicky ran away to live on the streets. He joined the notorious Brooklyn Mau-Mau gang and quickly became their warlord. He descended into a maelstrom of drugs, alcohol, and brutality, which worsened after a fellow gang member, fatally stabbed and beaten, died in his arms. Nicky was arrested countless times, and a psychiatrist predicted he was headed to "jail, the electric chair, and hell."

When street preacher David Wilkerson told Nicky of God's enduring love, Nicky beat him, spat on him, and threatened his life. Wilkerson replied, "You could cut me up into 1,000 pieces. . . . Every piece will still love you."

Wilkerson's reply gained a foothold in Nicky's brain, and shortly afterward he and his gang showed up at a Wilkerson rally held in a boxing arena. Wilkerson preached on Christ's crucifixion and the love that led Him to the cross. The message grabbed Nicky's heart. As he described it, "I was choked up with pain . . . and tears began to come down and more tears and I was fighting and then I surrendered."

A few other Mau-Mau members were also converted that night, and the next day they went to the police station and turned in all their handguns, knives, and bricks. The stunned police said it was a good thing they didn't see the gang coming loaded with weapons or they probably would have opened fire.

Nicky left the gang, enrolled in Bible college, got married, and moved back to New York where he ran Teen Challenge, a program for troubled teens. He converted many of his old fellow Mau-Maus, including their new leader, and has since become a world-traveling evangelist, author, and head of Nicky Cruz Ministries.[10]

Where would Nicky Cruz be today had he not heard that sermon that night? Without the gospel being preached to him, he might never have found the faith in God that he has since passed on to thousands.

The apostle Paul said that "faith comes by hearing, and hearing by the word of God" (Rom. 10:17). He did not mean all who hear the Word of God become believers; rather he meant faith can't exist unless there's a message or report of facts and events that lead one to believe.

Paul was identifying a critical need in the life of a Christian—faith is generated by the hearing of God's Word. This is a powerful reason to make church attendance one of your highest priorities. The preaching of the Word is a catalyst God uses to grow your faith. If you never sit under the sound of the Word of God through preaching, you miss an important opportunity to receive and be moved by it.

Hearing the Word spoken and preached by others allows Scripture to reach you and fill you in an essential way. Studying the Word on your own is how you then anchor the spoken Word in your life. You don't grow your faith by putting your Bible by your bed at night. You don't grow your faith by some emotional experience. Instead, faith deepens through reading or hearing God's Word.

D. L. Moody said that he prayed for faith, and "thought that some day faith would come down and strike me like lightning. But faith did not seem to come. One day I read in the tenth chapter of Romans, 'Now faith cometh by hearing, and hearing by the Word of God.' . . . I now opened my Bible, and began to study, and faith has been growing ever since."[11]

When we hear the Word of God or read the Word of God and then respond to the Word of God, our faith grows. When God tells us to do something and we do it, we strengthen our faith—our ability to believe Him. We discover that He is for us and is directing us in the way we should go.

TO GROW OUR FAITH, WE NEED PROBLEMS

In his book *Waiting: Finding Hope When God Seems Silent*, author and pastor Ben Patterson tells a harrowing tale illustrating what it means to exercise faith against all human reason.

He and three friends were climbing the highest mountain in Yosemite National Park. As they ascended the final two thousand feet to the peak, the two more experienced climbers moved ahead of Ben and his partner. Desiring to show off, Ben looked for a shortcut to beat them to the top. Against the advice of his partner, he set out on his own. A half hour later he found himself trapped atop the Lyell Glacier, looking down at a sheer face of ice dropping several hundred feet at a sharp angle. Just across the crevice stood the safety of a rock, but he dared not risk reaching it.

It took an hour for the other three climbers to find him, trapped and unmoved on the glacier face. One of them stood on the rock he wanted to reach and, stretching out, chopped two small footholds into the ice face with his axe. He gave Ben these instructions:

> Step out from where you are and put your foot where the first foothold is. When your foot touches it, without a moment's hesitation swing your other foot across and land it on the next step. When you do that, reach out and I will take your hand and pull you to safety. . . . As you step across, do not lean into the mountain! If anything, lean out a bit. Otherwise, your feet may fly out from under you and you will start sliding down.

Ben's natural instinct was to hug the ice face—to lean into the ice, not away from it. But in that desperate situation he was forced to make a choice. Would he lean on his own understanding or trust the wisdom of his friend? Two seconds later, his faith was rewarded and he was safe.

For a moment, based solely on what I believed to be true about the good will and good sense of my friend, I decided to say no to what I felt, to stifle my impulse to cling to the security of the mountain, to lean out, step out, and traverse the ice to safety.

To wait on God is to entrust your life to God in that way. The big difference is that the step of trust is a lifetime in the taking. It is a daily choice.[12]

None of us wants problems. We want life to be smooth sailing. We want happy relationships, fulfilling jobs, great health, and obedient children. Problems get in the way of all that, don't they? They hit us like storms, bringing waves of fear and disruption.

But problems drive us to the Lord and teach us to lean on Him. They can grow our confidence in the unseen reality of God and His involvement in our lives.

As pastor Tim Keller has written:

Believers understand many doctrinal truths in the mind, but those truths seldom make the journey down into the heart except through disappointment, failure, and loss. As a man who seemed about to lose both his career and his family once said to me, "I always knew, in principle, that 'Jesus is all I need' to get through. But you don't really know Jesus is all you need until Jesus is all you have."[13]

Our default tendency is to trust in ourselves and lean on our own understanding. But when we encounter a problem that's bigger than our ability to handle—that's when we learn our own resources are inadequate and that we can't truly rely on Jesus until we stop trying to rely only on ourselves.

God uses our problems to deepen our faith in Him. Life's most challenging and fearful situations can be our best opportunities to realize God's strength.[14] Ideally, we will reach out to Jesus as a first resort, not the last. But by His astounding love and grace, Jesus accepts us whenever we turn to Him.

The Reuters News Agency reported the story of Mark Ashton-Smith, a thirty-three-year-old lecturer at Cambridge University in England, who was kayaking alone in turbulent waters off the Isle of Wight. His kayak capsized, and he quickly realized he could not right his craft and make it to shore. Floating amidst the chopping waves, Mark's first instinct was to use his cell phone to call his father for help—even though his father was 3,500 miles away in Dubai, training British troops. Mark reached his father, who immediately relayed his son's situation to the coast guard base nearest to where the kayak had capsized—fortunately less than a mile away. Within twelve minutes a coast guard helicopter was on the scene and rescued Ashton-Smith.

We want to be like Mark Ashton-Smith—someone whose first thought is to exercise faith in our Father when we find ourselves facing a problem we can't solve.

TO GROW OUR FAITH, WE NEED PEOPLE

We're exploring Paul's command to overcome fear by "taking the shield of faith with which you will be able to quench all the fiery darts of the wicked one" (Eph. 6:16). Too often, however, modern Christians believe they are supposed to take up that shield on their own. But this metaphor is bigger than that.

While the Roman shield was carried by an individual soldier, it was most effective when combined with the shields of other soldiers. As the soldiers marched forward in a tight, organized cluster, their shields overlapped and interlocked to prevent points of entry for an enemy arrow. This was called the tortoise or phalanx formation.

"Do you see the critical point here?" wrote Stu Weber. "This is the shield of faith, which, by design, is interlocked with the soldier next to you. This is the shield of faith utilized in community, the community of faith. In our spiritual battles, as is true in any combat environment, there is no room for lone rangers. If you expect to be protected, you've got to stick with the group, march with the unit, and live like a family."[15]

Sometimes God strengthens us when we're all alone in the quiet of our room. But often He strengthens our faith through the words or presence of other people in our lives. So don't neglect the benefit of following Jesus as part of a community. Put yourself into a community of believers, and let God grow your faith alongside, and as part of, His people.

Dietrich Bonhoeffer put it this way:

> God put this Word into the mouth of human beings so that it may be passed on to others. When people are deeply affected by the Word, they tell it to other people. . . . Christians need other Christians who speak God's Word to them. They need them again and again when they become uncertain and disheartened. . . . They need other Christians as bearers and proclaimers of the divine word of salvation.[16]

The story of Jesus healing a paralytic in Mark 2:1–12 is a classic example of the power of combined faith. Jesus was in Capernaum, teaching in a house. The crowd was standing-room-only and multiple layers deep, overflowing the house and filling the yard. How would a paralyzed man ever reach Jesus in that crowd? He wouldn't on his own.

Fortunately this man had four friends who believed Jesus would heal him. They put their faith into remarkable action by lowering their paralyzed friend through the roof into the room below where Jesus sat teaching. Then we find this key statement in verse 5: "When Jesus saw *their* [plural] faith . . ." (emphasis added), He healed the man!

We can ask speculative questions all day long about how Jesus might have responded if only the paralytic had faith, if there had been only one, two, or three friends instead of four. That's a fool's errand. What we read is what we get: Jesus liked the faith-in-action of this group of five people, one sick and four helping, who locked their shields of faith together. This is the power of symbiosis—the whole being greater than the sum of the parts.

On January 25, 1736, an unconverted (or at least only nominally Christian) John Wesley was aboard a ship crossing the Atlantic Ocean with a group of Moravian missionaries—a fearless and faithful band of Christians. Their ship had already been battered by three storms, and now a fourth, more powerful than any of the others, was on the verge of sinking it. Wesley was petrified. He scribbled in his journal, "Storm greater: afraid!"

By contrast, the German Moravians had turned the below-deck area into a praise and worship service. As the waves crashed over the ship, they sang, not missing a beat, while Wesley stared at their composure in disbelief. After the storm passed, Wesley questioned their leader: "Were you not afraid?"

"No."

"Were your women and children not afraid?"

"No."

Wesley realized this community of Moravian missionaries had something he did not: a collective faith that could shield him against any fear—even the threat of death.

A little over two years later, in 1738, Wesley found that genuine faith while in a Moravian meeting in London. He became a pillar of fearless faith who still inspires us today.

One of the biggest weaknesses of modern, Western Christianity is our focus on individual salvation without a parallel focus on integration into the body of Christ. God never intended for people to follow Christ alone. To grow a faith that dispels your fears, you need other people. Faith is contagious!

If your faith is strong, consider if God is calling you to mentor those whose faith is young or weak. If your faith is weak or flagging in the face of extreme challenges, seek the encouragement and example of those with strong faith. Living as an isolated Christian makes growth in faith difficult, if not impossible.

TO GROW OUR FAITH, WE NEED PURPOSE

Daniel Ritchie was born without arms. It was challenging enough learning to function by using his feet and toes to dress and groom himself, eat, open doors, and drive. But he did it. His greater challenge, however, was dealing with the attitudes projected toward him. He endured stares, insults, and rudeness. His family was even asked to leave a restaurant because his eating with his feet offended other diners. The worst was the assumption, sometimes expressed directly, that he was a hopeless mistake—a misfit woefully insufficient to lead a full life.

As a result, Daniel came to believe that assumption. He developed a hatred for himself and for the people who disdained him.

Daniel Ritchie was not a Christian and had almost no friends. But one night a classmate invited him to church. That evening, the preacher gave a simple devotional on the love of God for all people. He quoted Psalm 139:14: "I will praise You, for I am fearfully and wonderfully made; marvelous are Your works." The message penetrated Daniel's heart. He realized God created him for a purpose, and he, too, was a marvelous work of God, every bit as much as those who had arms.

That night Daniel Ritchie gave his life to Christ; shortly afterward, he felt called to ministry. He now preaches and speaks at churches, conferences, and youth events in the US and abroad. As he puts it, he uses his empty sleeves to point people toward God.[17]

In 1787, God gave the devout British Christian Thomas Clarkson what seemed like an impossible project: to fight the slave trade in England.

Clarkson and a dozen others, including William Wilberforce, founded the Committee on Slave Trade and dedicated themselves to gathering intelligence, distributing pamphlets, delivering lectures, printing posters, recruiting advocates, and other activities to expose the inhumanity and brutality of slavery. Their God-inspired purpose was to build momentum to ban the slave trade in Britain.

Clarkson became the committee's only full-time anti-slavery campaigner and investigator. He traveled around the country gathering evidence for Wilberforce to use in Parliament. His task was not only extremely difficult, it was also incredibly dangerous. The opposition was overwhelming, given that much of England's economy depended on the slave trade. The country's prominent officials supported slavery, and public opinion was apathetic. As a result, Clarkson was shunned and ostracized. He received numerous death threats and at least one actual attempt on his life. In the darkest days of the campaign, he wrote, "I began now to tremble, for the first time, at the arduous task I had undertaken. . . . I questioned whether I should even get out of it alive."

But Clarkson's faith held firm. Through faith that God had called him to this work, he persevered. Soon he and his colleagues began to see a change. Petitions were circulated that collected thousands of signatures; books were published; boycotts against goods produced by slavery succeeded; and within five years, public opinion had completely turned against the slave trade.

Victory in Parliament took longer, but after several years of repeated defeats, Wilberforce's bill banning the slave trade passed in 1807. It had been a grueling project for Thomas Clarkson, but by holding firmly to his shield of faith, he was rewarded to see the completion of the task to which God had set him.[18]

God often gives us a purpose that requires us to trust in Him in special ways. That's one reason why Jesus loved to give His disciples tasks and challenges to build their faith. He sent them out two by two to preach and cast out demons and heal the sick. On one occasion He commanded them to feed five thousand people with only five loaves of bread and two fish—and on another to feed four thousand with seven loaves and a few small fish. And then at the end of His earthly ministry, He sent them ahead to Jerusalem to wait to be empowered by the Holy Spirit.

Giving us a sense of purpose is His way of stretching and strengthening our faith muscles.

TO GROW OUR FAITH, WE NEED PERSPECTIVE

When the disciples asked Jesus to increase their faith, He answered by telling them that if their faith was as small as a mustard seed, they would be able to uproot and cast a mulberry tree into the sea (Luke 17:5–6). In other words, the important issue was not the size of their faith; it was the size of their God.

Jesus' disciples needed the proper perspective in order to grow their faith. So do we.

I get an object lesson on perspective whenever I drive my car. With power steering, I can easily turn my two-ton automobile around with one finger—not because my finger is that strong, but because the power steering is. My finger merely acts to engage the power that accomplishes the task.

That's how faith works.

LifeStyle Ministries founder Ron Dunn said it this way:

Faith must have an object. To many people, the important thing is to believe and what you believe is secondary. They have the notion that there is something mystical, magical in the mere act of believing, a sort of holy *shazam* that transforms simple mortals into Captain Marvels. But the truth is, faith itself has no power. It is not faith that moves mountains, it is God. . . . Biblically speaking, faith, as a mere human activity, possesses no virtue, holds no merit, contains no power. The power of faith lies in its object.[19]

It's significant that the writer of Hebrews, after celebrating the faith of extraordinary believers in chapter 11, told us to "[fix] our eyes on Jesus, the author and perfecter of faith" (12:2, NASB). For our faith to be effective, we must keep our focus on Him.

In 1991, in the buildup of US and coalition troops prior to the First Gulf War, General Charles Krulak of the US Marine Corps was responsible for providing logistical support for eighty thousand marines moving into Kuwait. The site for their base was chosen because it was an old airfield that had the ability to provide 100,000 gallons of fresh water per day. As it has for centuries, fighting in the desert succeeds or fails based on the availability of water.

Fourteen days before the war was to begin, the commander in chief of the Coalition forces, General Norman Schwarzkopf, implemented a new tactical plan of attack. It required creating a new base for the marines and finding a new supply of water. But there was no water to be had in the new location!

For two weeks General Krulak had military engineers dig exploratory wells; he queried the Saudi government, the Kuwaiti government, local Bedouin tribes, and nomads as to any available supplies of water in the new location. The answer was the same from all sources: there was no water.

A committed Christian, General Krulak prayed daily in his devotional time for God to provide water for his troops. On the Sunday before the invasion, he was called out of a chapel service by one of his staff officers who needed to show him something. They drove down a road that Krulak's marines had built, a road he'd driven down at least seventy times, a road where at least sixty thousand marines had passed—and stopped.

His officer directed his attention to a spot twenty yards off the roadside where he saw something new: a fifteen-foot-tall pipe with two large hoses connected at the top. At the bottom was a giant diesel engine, a pump, and a five-hundred-gallon tank filled with diesel fuel. They walked to the spot, incredulous at what they were seeing. General Krulak pushed the diesel engine's On button and it roared to life, shooting fresh water out of the two hoses. His men measured the discharge rate of the water: 100,000 gallons a day—exactly what was required.

The marines didn't use diesel equipment; they had no diesel fuel. General Krulak had no idea how the well, the pump, and the fuel had materialized at exactly the right time, providing exactly the right amount of water. A reporter from the *London Times*, covering the buildup to the war, wrote an article that ran on the front page of the world-renowned paper: "The Miracle Well."

After retiring from the military as the commandant of the entire Marine Corps, General Krulak (among other post-retirement ventures) served as the president of a small liberal arts college. A friend of mine is an alumnus of that college who happened to read about General Krulak's "miracle well" around 2013. He wrote to General Krulak to inquire whether he ever learned the source of the well. The general responded no—he never learned where it came from. He still counts it as a miraculous answer to prayer.[20]

You and I may never need to find thousands of gallons of water each day for an army of eighty thousand soldiers in the middle of the desert. But General Krulak's faith gives us a new perspective on the meaning of "shield of faith." When we see God honoring faith at that level of need, we're encouraged to trust God for our needs as well. Problems are not big or small in God's sight. It's our perspective that needs enlarging so we see God as capable of responding to the faith we have.

No matter how small or insufficient you think your faith is, keep praying and trusting and seeking the Lord. Remember, it's the object of your faith—almighty God—not the size of your faith that's important. As you shift your focus from yourself to Him, your faith will grow and you will become fearless.

In God I have put my trust; I will not fear.

—Psalm 56:4

CHAPTER 7

OVERCOMING CONFUSION WITH WISDOM

As Staff Sergeant Thalamus Lewis made his way through a village in eastern Afghanistan on October 4, 2012, he heard bursts of gunfire. A single round from an enemy rifle struck him in the head, knocking him off the side of the road. "It was like a flash bang or something," he later said.

Lewis was stunned, his ears ringing and his head aching. And yet, somehow, he was alive. But it wasn't somehow; it was his ACH—his Advanced Combat Helmet. Back in the medical facility on base, he learned how efficiently his bulletproof helmet had saved him from certain death.

"Once they told me I took a round to the ACH, my first thing was I want to see it," he said. Inspecting the damaged helmet, he said in thankful amazement, "It actually works."

Lewis, who completed four combat deployments in his twenty years in the US Army, said he used to resent the weight and bulkiness of his equipment. "Being a soldier, we complain about a lot of stuff;

123

this gear was one of my main things when we deployed. I don't complain about it anymore. I am a walking testament."[1]

THE HELMET OF SALVATION

Like Sergeant Lewis, the apostle Paul understood the critical importance of the helmet. Crisscrossing the nations of the Roman Empire throughout his ministry, Paul saw the helmets of Roman soldiers everywhere.

In the Roman army, helmets of common soldiers were made of hardened leather. Officers' helmets could be augmented with metal; senior officers' helmets were topped by plumed crests. All served the same purpose as today's counterparts: to protect the skull and brain from blows inflicted by the enemy.

The helmet first became a metaphor for salvation in Isaiah 59:17, where it referred to the salvation Christ would bring to humanity. In Ephesians 6:17, Paul picked up this metaphor when he said to Christians, "And take the helmet of salvation."

In Ephesians, Paul was writing to believers—people who'd already received salvation. So the purpose of the spiritual helmet was not to impart salvation but to protect the believer's assurance of it. This assurance gives believers courage to fight their spiritual battles against mankind's great deceiver. This idea is reinforced in 1 Thessalonians 5:8, where Paul called the helmet "the *hope* of salvation" (emphasis added).

Just as a physical helmet protects a soldier's brain, the spiritual helmet protects your mind from the assaults of Satan's lies, corrupt philosophies, and confusion of thought—the weapons he uses to undermine your commitment and conviction of security in Christ.

What does the metaphor of the helmet represent? In short, it means to put on Christ, an idea found in Paul's epistles (Rom. 13:14; Gal. 3:27). When you put on Christ, you allow Him to live His life in and through you by the power of the Spirit.

More specifically, the helmet is a metaphor for the mind of Christ. Paul called Christ "the wisdom of God" (1 Cor. 1:24) and "wisdom from God" (v. 30).

From your reading of the four Gospels, can you remember a time when Christ was confused about anything? Was He ever puzzled or undone by what was happening around Him—by the words or actions of others? Was He confused by what God allowed to come into His life? Your answer should be, "No!"

Even in moments of extreme stress—like in the Garden of Gethsemane or when hanging on the cross—Jesus was not confused. In His humanity, He may have been in pain, even sorrow, at times. But He was never confused. He understood God's plan and will for His life because He had the wisdom of God. He *was* the wisdom of God.

When you put on this helmet, you put on the assurance of your own salvation, and you protect your mind from Satan's deceptions with the wisdom of God. This wisdom comes to you through the person of Jesus Christ. The Bible says, "But of Him you are in Christ Jesus, who became for us wisdom from God" (1 Cor. 1:30).

The wisdom of God equips and prepares you for God's purposes. It strengthens you in the certainty of your salvation so you can overcome confusion, falsehood, and uncertainty with the God-given confidence that comes through Christ alone.

You can live the same kind of life of confidence that our Lord lived. There may be times when you're uncomfortable, in pain, and even sorrowful. But with the wisdom of God—which you gain by putting on the helmet of your salvation—you can overcome confusion.

THE WISDOM OF THE OVERCOMER

After many years of struggling with infertility, Anthony Selvaggio and his wife decided to pursue adoption. Little did they know their journey would teach them as much about wisdom as love. After four-teen months of waiting, in November 2004, they received word from their adoption agency that a baby girl was waiting for them in China. A few weeks later, they boarded a plane to get her.

On their flight across the Pacific, they rehearsed all they had done to prepare for the moment they would officially become parents. They had read books and discussed good parenting strategies with family and friends. They had a game plan ready that would ensure a smooth transition for them and their new baby girl. Although a little nervous, Anthony and his wife thought they were prepared for whatever could come next.

A few days after arriving in China, they made their way to an old government building in the city of Wuhan. There, a beautiful fourteen-month-old girl was placed in their arms. Their dream had come true; they were parents at last! With hearts bursting with joy and gratitude, they returned to their hotel, ready to embark on the journey of a lifetime.

And that's when their new daughter, "so cute and charming, started to cry."

> At first, we responded fairly well. We had a strategy for crying. Got it right out of a book. So we applied the strategy—some cuddles, some rocking, a pacifier, that sort of thing. No effect. We applied it again. Again, no effect. None at all.
>
> Variations on the strategy didn't work, either. We were impro-vising freely now. . . . The minutes dragged on, slowing to a crawl as our baby's pitiable, heart-wrenching cries filled every corner of the room. Glancing at one another, my wife and I acknowledged the trace of panic we saw in each other's eyes. For here we were in a foreign country, far away from friends and family, with an utterly inconsolable baby girl who was now our sole responsibility. As the minutes stretched into hours, and the awful wailing settled down

into recurrent bouts of miserable sobbing, all our preparation and accumulated knowledge about parenthood began to seem completely worthless. Apparently, raising children was going to require more than knowledge.[2]

WISDOM IS ABOUT PRACTICE

Wisdom is often confused with knowledge, but there's a big difference. Knowledge involves the accumulation of facts. Wisdom is the ability to apply knowledge to achieve the best outcome. Knowledge is knowing that a tomato is a fruit, not a vegetable. Wisdom is knowing not to put a tomato in a fruit salad.

To protect our minds from deception and confusion, we need the wisdom dispensed by God Himself. That means we have to take the concept of wisdom further, because it's not enough for us to have only the wisdom the world offers.

In Scripture, wisdom refers to knowing the course of action that will please God and make our lives what He wants them to be. When God promises wisdom, He promises a way of life superior to the way of the world. He guarantees that through His gift of wisdom we will find that good and acceptable and perfect will of God (Rom. 12:2).

Wisdom is acquired through our efforts to learn, grow, improve, and study. It's not automatic, and it's not instantaneous.

Harvey Penick coached the golf team at the University of Texas from 1931 to 1963. He was a mentor and instructor to many professional golfers who sought his advice on their game.

In working with golfers—whether amateurs or professionals—Penick was a keen observer. For decades he collected observations about golf in a notebook. If he saw something that worked, he wrote it down; if he saw something that didn't work, he wrote that down too. After retiring, he mentioned his golf diaries to a writer, who recognized their potential.

In 1992, when Penick was eighty-seven years old, *Harvey Penick's*

Little Red Book: Lessons and Teachings from a Lifetime in Golf was published. Four more books followed, three posthumously based on his notes. The *Little Red Book* remains the bestselling book on golf ever published and is still in print today.

Could Harvey Penick have written that book in 1931? No, because it took decades of coaching and observing to gain his wisdom. Wisdom comes from living and learning, from a hunger to learn and grow over the course of a lifetime. The more you humble yourself and keep a hungry heart, the more wisdom you'll acquire.

WISDOM IS ABOUT PERSPECTIVE

There's another misunderstanding as to what this gift of wisdom really means and how we apply it in our lives. In his book *Knowing God*, J. I. Packer uses a vivid metaphor that helps explain it. Imagine you're in a train station, standing on the end of a platform and watching the constant movement of trains coming in and going out. From this limited perspective, your vision and comprehension of the overall working of the train system is almost nonexistent.

Now imagine you go into the station's control center. A long, electronic wall chart with a diagram of the entire system shows all the tracks extending five miles on either side of the station. By following the little lights moving on the chart, you can locate each train with all its cars and see exactly where it's headed. As you watch the system through the eyes of the men who control it, you understand why trains are stopped and started, diverted and sidetracked. The logic behind every movement becomes clear when you see the entire picture.[3]

The mistake many Christians make when seeking wisdom is to assume that, once found, it will enable them to see life from the control center instead of the train platform. I've heard it described as "getting God's perspective on our world."

But that's not how wisdom works in the Christian life. We're not shown the overall pattern of the universe or exactly how our lives fit into it. We're not shown God's long-term plan for us or how our actions today will play into that plan tomorrow, next year, or in the next generation. But when we humble ourselves, desire God's wisdom, and listen to His words and obey them, He gives us all the wisdom we need for the moment—the wisdom simply to take the next step. That's all we need to face the present situation and make the right decision.

Being an Overcomer isn't something we accomplish by our own power and wisdom. When we can't see how our everyday decisions and actions fit into God's cosmic plan, God essentially says to us, "Let Me relieve you of that worry, that fear. Just take this one little step into the light I have placed in front of you, and I will see to it that your faithful action will fit into the overarching plan and accomplish both My goals and your good."

WISDOM IS ABOUT PATIENCE

In 1939, at age twenty-seven, John Templeton borrowed $10,000 from his boss and bought shares in 104 companies with a stock price of less than $1.00 per share. Several of those companies were even in bankruptcy, but Templeton was buying for the long term. He believed those companies would bounce back. Almost all of them did. Four years later he sold all those stocks for more than $40,000—a quadruple return on his initial investment. Sir John Templeton went on to become one of history's greatest investors and philanthropists; he was also a committed Christian. He had an uncanny ability to trust in the long view of life, and a deep commitment to joy, positivity, and love—all characteristics of the world's wisest people.[4]

Although we can't always see how all the details of our lives fit together, God has revealed to us the ending of our story. In spite of the confusion around us, we keep our eyes on the prize—the hope of our future eternal salvation through Christ—and we navigate life in light of eternity. In more mundane terms, to live wisely means we live with the big picture in mind, no matter what comes at us.

Life can be filled with love, beauty, joy, and understanding. It can also bring us one obstacle, temptation, or crisis after another. People with different goals and standards may use or delude us, but some will help us if we let them. Some offer temptation; others offer support. At times we can be deeply confused, feeling like pursued animals seeking refuge but wondering if the sanctuary we're heading for is really a trap.

God promises to give us wisdom to overcome this daily confusion and to learn to respond as He directs us through every situation. We become clear-sighted and realistic, looking at life as it is and making decisions that keep us on the right path. The broad outlines of cause and effect and the shape of the future are God's to fully understand, and God's alone. But the way through our lives becomes clear as we live with the end in mind.

Now you can stand firm against the attacks of the devil because you have put on God's truth, His righteousness, His peace, His faithfulness, His salvation, and His Word. You have all the dimensions of the armor of God because you are clothed with Christ.

GET WISDOM

In one way or another, most of us have asked God for guidance and wisdom at some point. Does "Lord, help me know what to do?" sound familiar? You're not alone. Many pastors I know pray for wisdom as part of their daily routine.

If you sense that need in your life, as I do in mine, let's learn together how wonderfully open God is to dispensing His wisdom to those who seek Him.

Some years ago I was challenged to read through the book of Proverbs each month. Since there are thirty-one chapters in the book, reading a chapter each day took me through the entire collection of wise sayings twelve times that year. I've never regretted that time spent in the Proverbs.

One of the early discoveries of my study was the many promises God has given to those who seek after and obtain His wisdom.

- "Happy is the man who finds wisdom, and the man who gains understanding" (Prov. 3:13).
- "For wisdom is better than rubies, and all the things one may desire cannot be compared with her" (Prov. 8:11).
- "When wisdom enters your heart, and knowledge is pleasant to your soul, discretion will preserve you; understanding will keep you" (Prov. 2:10–11).

Over and over Solomon said, "Get wisdom." The question is, how do we get it?

HOW THE OVERCOMER ACQUIRES WISDOM

As I studied this question and read and reread the Word of God in search of the answer, I began to see some consistent patterns. Our ability to acquire God's wisdom is not so much a matter of doing as it is of being. It isn't so much an activity as it is an attitude.

I once heard a preacher say that our attitude determines our altitude. When it comes to climbing the heights of God's wisdom, there's truth in that statement. To use a more down-to-earth metaphor, He is eager to plant the seeds of His wisdom in us, but before those seeds can take root, we must prepare the ground of our minds to receive them. We prepare by adopting four basic attitudes: the humility to hear God's wisdom, hunger to seek God's wisdom, hearing to truly listen to God's wisdom, and a heeding heart to follow God's wisdom.

A HUMBLE SPIRIT

The first step in acquiring wisdom is a proper understanding of one's relationship to God. Solomon put it this way: "The fear of the LORD is the beginning of knowledge, but fools despise wisdom and instruction" (Prov. 1:7). Job answered his own quest for wisdom with the same basic conclusion: "Behold, the fear of the Lord, that is wisdom" (Job 28:28).

What does it mean to fear the Lord? Does God really want us to tremble and quake in terror before Him?

Pastor and scholar Sinclair Ferguson describes the fear of God as "that indefinable mixture of reverence, fear, pleasure, joy and awe which fills our hearts when we realize who God is and what He has done for us."[5]

Another scholar wrote, "To fear Yahweh is to stand in a subservient position to him, to acknowledge one's dependence upon him."[6]

My interest in the subject of God's wisdom came at a time when I was making a major change in my own life and ministry. It was a humbling experience that caused me to depend on God in new and profound ways. After starting and pastoring a church for some twelve years, I sensed God leading me to a new assignment.

Each week, as I learned more about the challenge and responsibility of God's new calling in my life, I sensed a growing feeling of despair. The words of Paul described my attitude all too well: "Who is sufficient for these things?" (2 Cor. 2:16).

When we are overwhelmed and confused in any area of life, the book of James says our task is to pray and ask God for guidance: "If any of you lacks wisdom, let him ask of God, who gives to all liberally and without reproach, and it will be given to him" (1:5). And so I prayed for God's wisdom to calm my mind and clarify my path so that I might achieve His purpose. In a short time, that clarity came and confusion left me. My way was clear to me. You can imagine how encouraged I was to realize that my earlier fear and despair were merely stepping-stones to the help I needed from God.

Billy Graham tells the story of a young company president who prayed on his knees in his office every morning. His secretary knew to deflect any visitors until his daily "appointment" was concluded. When the chairman of the company's board wanted to see the president immediately, the secretary's attempts to postpone the meeting were futile. The chairman stormed into the president's office and found him on his knees in prayer. He withdrew quietly and asked the secretary, "Is this normal?" "Every day," she said. To which the chairman answered, "No wonder I come to him for advice."[7]

The prophet Jeremiah wrote:

> "Let not the wise man glory in his wisdom, let not the mighty man glory in his might, nor let the rich man glory in his riches; but let him who glories glory in this, that he understands and knows Me, that I am the LORD, exercising lovingkindness, judgment, and righteousness in the earth. For in these I delight," says the LORD. (Jer. 9:23–24)

A person who is wise according to God's definition knows too well his own weaknesses. He never assumes infallibility. He who knows most knows how little he knows.[8] That's what it means to have a humble spirit, which is the first step in opening oneself to God's gift of wisdom.

A HUNGRY SOUL

Imagine the company you work for suddenly transfers you to a Middle Eastern country to set up a branch office. Time is of the essence, so you make the move.

Quickly you realize what a beautiful and gracious people surround you, yet you can barely find your way around. Finding a place to live, learning about the currency, trying new foods, embarrassing yourself with the language—you suffer through it all, constantly making mistakes.

You and your company both have a lot riding on this move. Determined to be successful, you attend immersive language classes, hire a "cultural coach," and use translation software to read about banking, driving, shopping, and cultural norms. Gradually, you acquire the skills and knowledge to succeed in your work.

A year later, coworkers from America join you. They're amazed at how wise you've become in the ways of your new culture. But you know it was only because you were hungry to succeed!

Something similar happens to you when you become a Christian. You're transferred from the kingdom of darkness to the kingdom of light; from the kingdom of this world to the kingdom of God (Col. 1:13). It happens overnight when you are born again through faith in Christ. Your new home requires the acquisition of new skills and a new perspective. The hungrier you are to make a success of this "new venture," the sooner you'll learn to live skillfully and successfully in God's kingdom.

Wisdom must be sought in order to be found; it doesn't arrive wrapped in a bow on the doorstep of your Christian life.

A. W. Tozer made much of the hunger factor. He wrote, "The great people of the Bible and Christian history have had an insatiable hunger for God. He wants to be wanted. Too bad that with many of us He waits so long, so very long in vain."[9]

This is not just a modern problem. Five hundred years before Tozer, Lady Julian of Norwich asked, "God, of your goodness, give me yourself for you are enough for me. If I ask for anything less I know I shall continue to want. Only in you I have everything."[10]

We have as much of God and His wisdom as we want to have. Our lack of wisdom is the result of our own lack of desire to know more of God and to know Him with all our heart. Do you seek to know God with all your heart?

In one psalm alone, Psalm 119, we're instructed to seek God with our whole heart six different times in six different phrasings. We're told to . . .

- keep God's testimonies with our whole heart (v. 2),
- seek God's commandments with our whole heart (v. 10),
- obtain God's Word with our whole heart (v. 34),
- entreat God's favor with our whole heart (v. 58),
- keep God's precepts with our whole heart (v. 69), and
- cry unto God with our whole heart (v. 145).

If whole-hearted seeking after God is a prerequisite for wisdom, many of us know where our problem lies: our desire for God is too weak. If we want more of God, we must increase our hunger for Him.

In his book *A Thirst for God*, Sherwood Wirt explains that physical and spiritual hunger are fundamentally different. When we're physically hungry, we eat and are satisfied. The hunger disappears.

But when we're spiritually hungry, we eat and find ourselves even hungrier. We discover that our appetite for God and His Word is increased. That's why disciplined, consistent study of God's Word and regular participation in a Bible-teaching ministry are critical for the growth of our spiritual lives as Christians.

But notice this: When we're physically hungry and miss a meal, we soon feel like we're starving and we can't wait to eat. In the spiritual realm, it's just the opposite. When we miss our spiritual meals, we begin to lose our appetites.[11]

We are in serious danger when we fail to demonstrate a soul that is hungry for God and His wisdom.

A HEARING HEART

As the 1944 presidential election approached, Franklin D. Roosevelt had been president for three terms. With the nation deeply involved in World War II, Roosevelt's health was failing and his advisors thought there was a good chance that, if re-elected, Roosevelt would die during his fourth term. That would leave his vice president, Henry Wallace, to guide the nation through the rest of the war—a man they didn't feel would be up to the task. So, for the 1944 election, Roosevelt made a little-known senator from Missouri, Harry S. Truman, his running mate. The Roosevelt-Truman ticket was elected easily.

Only three months into his fourth term, the worst happened: President Roosevelt died of a massive cerebral hemorrhage. Vice President Harry Truman, with less than three months of executive office experience under his belt, was suddenly the president of the United States. Only after being sworn into office did Truman learn the shocking news: America was in possession of an atomic bomb. Secrecy about the bomb project had excluded the vice president from the need-to-know circle during his first three months in office. Ironically, he became the president to use that bomb later that year in Japan to bring an end to the war.

When Truman met with reporters the day after taking office, he told them, "I don't know whether you fellows ever had a load of hay fall on you, but when they told me yesterday [about the president's death], I felt like the moon, the stars and the planets had fallen on me."

And a few days later, in his first address before a joint session of Congress, Truman expressed his dependence on God for wisdom in the face of his new responsibilities: "At this moment, I have a heart of prayer. As I have assumed my duties, I humbly pray to Almighty God in the words of King Solomon: 'Therefore give to Your servant an understanding heart to judge Your people, that I may discern between good and evil. For who is able to judge this great people of Yours?'"[12]

In 1 Kings 3:9, Solomon, in his unique supplication to God, asked for an understanding heart. The text literally says, "Give therefore Your servant a *hearing* heart."

What a request! A hearing heart. Although we may have a humble spirit and a hungry soul, we still must learn to listen. We must be sensitive to what God may say to us through His Word and through His people as they share the principles of His wisdom.

Once again, we turn to Proverbs to learn the virtue of good listening:

- "A wise man will hear and increase learning, and a man of understanding will attain wise counsel, to understand a proverb and an enigma, the words of the wise and their riddles" (Prov. 1:5–6).
- "Listen to counsel and receive instruction, that you may be wise in your latter days" (19:20).
- "Incline your ear and hear the words of the wise, and apply your heart to my knowledge; for it is a pleasant thing if you keep them within you; let them all be fixed upon your lips" (22:17–18).

There's so much of God's wisdom all around us, available to us from those who have walked with God before us. But we have to train ourselves to listen.

It's easy to find courses and seminars guaranteed to make us better speakers. But where are the courses designed to make us better listeners? We give our graduates awards for good speaking, but I've never seen an award for excellent listening.

God gave us two ears and one mouth for a reason. Yet for most of us, the mouth is greatly overworked, while the ears are in a state of semi-retirement. One man explained it this way: "A wise man talks because he has something to say. Fools talk because they have to say something."

Charles Bridges reminds us of an important point: "We gather knowledge when we listen; we spend it when we teach; but if we spend before we gather, we'll soon be bankrupt.[13]

A HEEDING MIND

A humble spirit says, "I need God." A hungry soul says, "I desire God." A hearing heart says, "I will listen to God." And finally, a heeding mind says, "I will obey God."

To know that we need God is important. To reach out for Him is imperative. To hear what He has to say is crucial. But it's all meaningless unless we determine to do what He tells us.

Moses affirmed the principle of acting on what God tells us in his final address to the Israelites, whom he led for forty years:

> Surely I have taught you statutes and judgments, just as the LORD my God commanded me, that you should act according to them in the land which you go to possess. Therefore be careful to observe them; for this is your wisdom and your understanding in the sight of the peoples who will hear all these statutes, and say, "Surely this great nation is a wise and understanding people." (Deut. 4:5–6)

We're not wise because we have God's Word. We're not wise because we desire God's Word. We're not even wise because we read God's Word. We're wise only when we keep and obey God's Word.

Several years ago, when I was invited to speak in a church in West Virginia, a member of that congregation took me to tour a coal mine. Before being lowered into the mine shaft, he gave me a carbide lamp that miners wear as headgear.

When we were deep in the mine, he signaled to the surface control center to turn off all the lights in the shaft. I've never been in such darkness in my life. The only source of light was the small lamp I wore on my head, which emitted a short beam that illuminated only a step or two in front of me. I remember being afraid to move at first. I could see nothing on either side and very little ahead.

But I soon made a significant discovery. As soon as I walked into the light that I did have, that light projected the way for an additional step into the darkness. As long as I kept moving forward, so did the light, which meant there was always enough light on my pathway to keep me from stumbling and to guarantee my progress.

That small lamp on my head was my helmet of salvation. It showed me what I needed to see to move forward in the darkness. And as I moved forward, I brought the light with me.

BE FILLED WITH GOD'S WISDOM

Many years ago, I performed the wedding ceremony for two of the most remarkable young people I'd ever met. Bill and Rhonda were on the Navigator's staff at Indiana University in Bloomington, Indiana. Their wedding turned out to be a church service. They both gave dynamic testimonies of their relationship with the Lord and of His leading in their lives. To this day, when I officiate at a wedding, I remember theirs.

About two years after their wedding, I received a call from Bill telling me they'd just learned Rhonda had advanced leukemia. What a shock! We prayed together over the phone, and a few days later we got together to discuss the doctor's ominous prognosis.

For a brief time, Rhonda went into remission. But within a few months, her condition deteriorated again. Finally, she was admitted to the Indiana University Medical Center in Indianapolis.

I'll never forget the afternoon I flew to Indianapolis to visit her. My heart was heavy as I walked into her room. But when I left the hospital, I had the distinct impression that I'd been ministered to that day. Rhonda spent most of our visit sharing with me what God had been teaching her through His Word, as well as some of the verses she and Bill had been memorizing together.

A few days after my visit, Rhonda went home to be with the Lord. In the hour before she died, she recited many of the passages of God's

Word with which she had filled her life. According to the nurse who was with her when she died, "She went home to God in the middle of a verse."

What a way to die. Better yet, what a way to live! Being "filled with the knowledge of His will in all wisdom and spiritual understanding" (Col. 1:9).

Wisdom guides us in overcoming the confusing events of our lives—all of them. It is acting with skill on what is known and trusting God with what is unknown. When we put on the helmet of salvation, we move forward steadily in the light of His wisdom and we live as Overcomers.[14]

The fear of the LORD *is the beginning of wisdom; a good understanding have all those who do His commandments.*
—PSALM 111:10

CHAPTER 8

OVERCOMING TEMPTATION WITH SCRIPTURE

Basketball referee Al Covino was officiating a high school league championship game in New Rochelle, New York. New Rochelle was the home team, coached by Dan O'Brien; their opponent was Yonkers. The game was a back-and-forth nail-biter. As the clock ticked down to thirty seconds, Yonkers led by one point.

Yonkers shot and missed. New Rochelle grabbed the rebound and passed the ball up the court. The roar of the crowd was deafening as the New Rochelle player shot for the basket. The ball rolled tantalizingly around the rim and fell off. A teammate recovered it and quickly tapped it in for the apparent victory. The home crowd went wild.

Referee Covino looked at the clock and saw that time had expired. But he couldn't affirm New Rochelle's final basket because the crowd noise had prevented him from hearing the buzzer. He checked with the other official, but he hadn't heard it either. Covino approached the timekeeper, a boy of seventeen who gazed up at him with a long, sad face and said, "Mr. Covino, the buzzer went off as the ball rolled off the rim—before the final tap-in was made."

Covino had no choice but to tell Coach O'Brien that he'd lost the championship game. The coach was crestfallen. His face clouded over and his head drooped. At that moment the young timekeeper came up to him and said, "I'm sorry, Dad. I had to tell Mr. Covino the time ran out before the final basket."

O'Brien looked up at his son. The cloud passed from his face, and he brightened as if the sun had burst through. "That's okay, son," he said. "You did what you had to do. I am proud of you."

The coach turned to Covino and said proudly, "Al, I want you to meet my son, Joe." Then the two walked off the court, the father standing tall with his arm around his son's shoulders.[1]

Can you imagine the temptations that boy had to fight? It was his own school's championship game. He was the son of the coach. Only he knew the buzzer had sounded before the final basket. He held in his hands the key to the culmination of the team's entire successful season. It would have been so easy to yield to the temptation to say the buzzer had sounded after that last shot instead of before. No one would have known the difference.

There was also another potential temptation—the coach's temptation to win at any cost. O'Brien could have said, "Son, how could you do this to me? To your team? To your school? You let us all down."

But neither father nor son yielded to these temptations, and I think we can see why. It's apparent in the pride the father showed in his son's integrity. The boy had been taught to do the right thing. Because of that, they lost the game but achieved a much bigger victory that day.

THE LURE OF TEMPTATION

Temptation. The lure of attraction, the pull toward pleasure, the seduction of the will to abandon what we know is right to indulge in the act of the moment that seems immediately satisfying. Ever since that fateful day in Eden, temptation has been the primary factor leading men and women away from God.

Temptation affects everyone. It doesn't matter who you are, how strong you are, how knowledgeable, how immersed in the Bible, or how committed to integrity.

To be Overcomers, we must constantly be on our guard because temptation is no respecter of persons.

I believe that sin has never been as accessible as it is now, and evil has never been so user-friendly. Our technologies, mixed with the sinful tendencies of our fallen nature and intensified by Satan, have put a capital *T* in Temptation. And our loss of a clear north star of morality and self-control has only made it worse.

It's not just the major red-letter temptations that assault us, for the daily stress of life today creates constant opportunities for us to yield to impatience, irritability, anxiety, profanity, and sharpness of tongue. Often the big sin is preceded by a lack of self-control in the small moments. If you choose not to control your impatience, how will you control your desire, anger, or greed?

Someone compared temptation to a rattlesnake—a deadly thing to get away from immediately when seen or heard. Oh, how I wish temptation were like a rattlesnake! Shunning and avoiding something so threatening and hideous is easy.

But we all know temptation isn't like that. It's more like a piece of chocolate cake, a hundred-dollar bill, a beautiful woman or handsome man, a pair of dice, a corner office, a new Lexus, or a chance to see the answers to the exam. Temptation is attractive; otherwise it wouldn't be tempting. And it's dangerous *because* it's attractive.

The Cueva de Villa Luz, or Cave of the Lighted House, is located in southern Mexico. The cave is a gorgeous paradise—a lush rain forest filled with colorful tropical birds, spectacular rock formations, and idyllic ponds. Twenty underground springs feed the cave, creating beautiful watercourses teeming with fish. The environment is enticing. Yet if you enter that cave, you'll soon be dead. It is filled with poisonous gases.[2]

That is the nature of temptation. It presents itself as beautiful and inviting. But behind that mask it's dangerous and deadly.

DON'T JUST WALK, RUN!

No doubt the best way to avoid temptation is to stay away from it. I like the story of a man who rushed in to his doctor and said, "Doc, I just broke my arm in two places." The doctor replied, "Well then, stay out of those places."

We laugh, but there's a truth here. Just because it seems obvious that we should avoid temptation doesn't mean we'll make it our habit to do so. We have to decide to avoid temptation, and then we must enforce that decision with our will. When we know our weaknesses and what tempts us, staying out of those places and situations is exactly what we should rigorously do.

Caution and care in guarding ourselves from what entices us is essential. Yet despite all our care and caution, we'll all be tempted at some point. It's part of life. Just remember that temptation itself is not sin. Yielding to temptation is!

J. Wilbur Chapman explains the difference, saying temptation is "the tempter looking through the keyhole into the room where you are living. Sin is your drawing back the bolt and making it possible for him to enter."[3]

As long as you live, you will be tempted. But whatever temptation you're going through, you're in good company. Someone around you right now is struggling with the same pressures you feel, and he probably thinks he's the only one facing that particular temptation. But that's not the case.

"No temptation has overtaken you except such as is common to man; but God is faithful, who will not allow you to be tempted beyond what you are able, but with the temptation will also make the way of escape, that you may be able to bear it" (1 Cor. 10:13).

Even Jesus faced temptation. Hebrews 4:15 says, "We do not have a High Priest who cannot sympathize with our weaknesses, but was in all points tempted as we are, yet without sin."

Remember that temptation never comes from God: "Let no one say when he is tempted, 'I am tempted by God'; for God cannot be tempted by evil, nor does He Himself tempt anyone" (James 1:13).

It's the devil who tempts us to evil; that's why he's called "the tempter" in Matthew 4:3 and 1 Thessalonians 3:5. If you've been a Christian for long, the tempter is no stranger to you. He roars about like a lion, seeking those to devour, and I'm sure he's passed your way more than once. But while you must respect and be wary of the devil's temptations, you don't need to have an inordinate fear of them.

Our faithful God won't allow us to be tempted beyond what we can bear. He may test us by allowing temptation, but He never tempts us Himself.

Warren Wiersbe wrote:

Jesus was not tempted so that the Father could learn anything about His Son, for the Father had already given Jesus His divine approval. Jesus was tempted so that every creature in heaven, on earth, or under the earth might know that Jesus Christ is the Conqueror. He exposed Satan and his tactics, and He defeated Satan. Because of His victory, we can have victory over the tempter.[4]

That was a key truth expressed by the author of Hebrews: "For in that He Himself has suffered, being tempted, He is able to aid those who are tempted" (2:18).

OVERCOMING TEMPTATION

As Paul told the Corinthians, when we're undergoing temptation, God always provides a way of escape. The phrase "way of escape" is translated from a Greek word that denotes a passageway out of a canyon. If you wandered into a ravine and couldn't see any way out, you might at first think you were trapped. But if you searched hard enough, you'd usually find a path somewhere—a way out.

We find our best escape route away from temptation by intentionally staying close to Christ. He resisted temptation in every circumstance, which means He always knows the way out of the canyon.[5]

As Overcomers, we've been warned that we're in a spiritual battle that demands special equipment. And our exploration of Ephesians 6 has revealed how wonderfully God has protected us by giving us exactly the equipment we need to wage this battle.

We've been well-supplied with the belt of truth. We're protected by the breastplate of righteousness. Our feet are shod with the preparation of the gospel of peace. We carry the shield of faith, with which we can deflect all the fiery darts of the evil one. Our heads are covered with the helmet of salvation, the wisdom of God for every situation.

Every piece of this armor has one thing in common: it is all defensive by design. Its purpose is to protect us from the attacks of the evil one.

In this chapter we will discover that the Lord has also given us an offensive weapon. It is "the sword of the Spirit, which is the word of God" (Eph. 6:17).

John MacArthur tells us that . . .

The Greek word [for "sword"] refers to a dagger anywhere from six to eighteen inches long. It was carried in a sheath or scabbard at the soldier's side and used in hand-to-hand combat. The sword of

146

the Spirit is not a broadsword you swing or flail around, hoping to do damage. It's incisive; it must hit a vulnerable spot or it won't be effective.[6]

In the rest of this chapter we'll explore and explain this sword of the Spirit, focusing on three significant topics that reveal its full meaning and purpose. First, I'll explain what this sword really is and how it works. Next, I'll reveal to you an example of One who wielded this sword with masterful precision. And finally, I'll explore ways you and I can benefit from "the sword of the Spirit, which is the word of God."

Let's begin with . . .

THE EXPLANATION

"And take . . . the sword of the Spirit, which is the word of God" (Eph. 6:17).

This passage leaves no ambiguity as to what the sword metaphor means for the Christian. The apostle Paul tells us plainly that the sword of the Spirit is the word of God. But there are two Greek terms commonly translated into English as "word." The first is *logos*, the more common of the two. It's used to describe the overarching revelation of God that we have in the Bible. It's an all-encompassing term denoting the whole of the Bible—what we often call God's Word. The Bible in its totality is the *logos* of God, as in: "Remember those who rule over you, who have spoken the word [*logos*] of God to you" (Heb. 13:7).

But *logos* is not the word we find in Ephesians 6:17.

The Greek term for "word" in Ephesians 6:17 is *rhema*. The *rhema* of God means "a saying of God." We could translate the verse this way: "Take the sword of the Spirit, which is a saying of God."

The difference between the *logos* of God and the *rhema* of God is critical to our understanding of this offensive weapon. *Logos* refers to the complete revelation of what God has said in the Bible. But *rhema* means a specific saying of God—a passage or verse drawn from the whole that has special application to an immediate situation.

Do you remember the "sword drills" that many churches used to train their youth groups? The teacher would suddenly cry, "Draw your swords!" like an army sergeant—or maybe more like a Roman centurion. Then he'd call out a Bible verse, and you'd scramble to find the passage in your Bible, your "sword." Indexed Bibles were not allowed, which meant that to be successful, students had to become quite familiar with the contents of the book.

When I was a child I thought the whole Bible was a sword. But the Bible is not the sword; the Bible is the armory filled with swords— filled with the sayings of God!

Please hear me carefully. I am not saying that the Bible *becomes* the Word of God when we use it a certain way. Some theologians teach that the Bible is just a book of literature, and that when you have a revelation about something it says, then at that moment it becomes *your* Word of God. You've made it the Word of God in your own mind by your interaction with it. Like the proverbial tree falling in the forest that makes no sound unless you are there to hear it, many believe the Bible has no special meaning except what you give it. Or it's like the psychological meaning of a Rorschach ink blot: it has whatever meaning your mind attributes to it.

That is heresy, and that is most certainly not what I am teaching.

The Bible is the Word of God whether we read it or not. It is the Word of God whether it means anything to us or not. It is the Word of God whether we ever feel anything when we read it, whether we even understand what we are reading. The Bible is God's Word, and nothing can change that!

But from this vast arsenal that is the Word of God, we find the specific sayings of God that are the swords He gives us to use in spiritual warfare.

Ray Stedman has a helpful word concerning the way the sword of the Spirit works in our lives. He wrote:

> Sometimes when you are reading a passage of Scripture, the words seem suddenly to come alive, take on flesh and bones, and leap off the page at you, or grow eyes that follow you around everywhere you go, or develop a voice that echoes in your ears until you can't get away from it. This is the rhema of God, the sayings of God that strike home like arrows to the heart. This is the sword of the Spirit which is the word of God.[7]

The person who uses the sword of the Spirit better than anyone else is the One who designed it: the Lord Jesus Christ. Let's look at how Jesus used Scripture to overcome temptation.

THE EXAMPLE

When Christ was tempted by the devil in the wilderness, He wielded the sword of the Spirit with the deftness and precision of an invincible warrior. His use of the sword provides us with the best example in all Scripture of how this powerful weapon is to be used.

To fully appreciate the circumstance and effectiveness of Christ's swordsmanship, we must first understand the nature of His temptation. We start with Matthew 3 and the account of His baptism. When Jesus emerged from the water after John baptized Him, God in heaven validated His Messiahship by declaring, "This is My beloved Son, in whom I am well pleased" (Matt. 3:17).

After that moment of validation, Satan attempted to trap Jesus in a phenomenon that is often described today as the Matterhorn

Syndrome. In Switzerland, there's a cemetery at the base of the Matterhorn filled primarily with bodies of climbers who died on this fourteen-thousand-foot mountain in the Alps. But strangely enough, the majority of those buried there were casualties on their way down the mountain—not on their way up. Having achieved their goal of reaching the top, they let down their guard and became careless in their descent.

Satan deviously chose to tempt Jesus after He had experienced one of His greatest moments while on this earth—the verbal declaration of His Father's pleasure in Him—which is what we might call a mountaintop experience. It was a time to watch out for the Matterhorn Syndrome.

In Matthew 4:1–11, we read that the Spirit led Jesus to the wilderness, where Satan tempted Him at the very heart of the Father's words. Near the end of Jesus' forty-day fast in the desert, Satan approached Him with three separate temptations. These three temptations comprise the enemy's strategy against humanity from the beginning of time. They are "the lust of the flesh, the lust of the eyes, and the pride of life" (1 John 2:16).

This was Satan's strategy in the garden of Eden. He told Eve the fruit was good for food (the lust of the flesh), pleasant to the eyes (the lust of the eyes), and able to make one wise (the pride of life). Let's look at how Satan employed these same temptations against Jesus in the wilderness—and how Jesus overcame them.

THE LUST OF THE FLESH

Matthew 4:1–3: "Then Jesus was led up by the Spirit into the wilderness to be tempted by the devil. And when He had fasted forty days and forty nights, afterward He was hungry. Now when the tempter came to Him, he said, 'If you are the Son of God, command that these stones become bread.'"

In this first temptation, Satan said to Jesus, "Why not satisfy Your hunger by performing a simple little miracle? If You are the Son of God, what's the harm in turning this little rock into a loaf of bread?"

Satan was tempting Jesus Christ to use His divine power to meet His human needs. He was trying to get Jesus to act independently of the Father, to contradict the Father's Word. As the Scottish theologian George MacDonald noted, "the Father had said, 'That is a stone.' Would the Son now say, 'That is a loaf'?"[8] Satan was playing on the human hunger of Jesus, trying to get Him to step outside the will of His Father and perform a miracle for Himself.

To overcome this first thrust of temptation, Jesus reached into His armory and pulled out a sword, a *rhema*: "He answered and said, 'It is written, "Man shall not live by bread alone, but by every word that proceeds from the mouth of God"'" (Matt. 4:4).

To overcome Satan, Jesus quoted Deuteronomy 8:3. The key word is *alone*. Man shall not live by bread alone—or by bread *only*. Jesus reminded Satan that feeding on and obeying God's Word is more important than eating and being nourished by physical food.

Here Jesus was saying bluntly, "Listen, Satan, it's God who keeps people alive, not bread. He knows His people's needs and He meets them. Just as He gave Israel manna in the Sinai wilderness, He will take care of Me in this wilderness. But He does it by giving Me more than bread; He gives me Himself through every act, every word. And that is all the nourishment I need."

THE LUST OF THE EYES

Matthew 4:5–6 continues the story: "Then the devil took Him up into the holy city, set Him on the pinnacle of the temple, and said to Him, 'If You are the Son of God, throw Yourself down. For it is written: "He shall give His angels charge over you," and, "In their hands they shall bear you up, lest you dash your foot against a stone."'"

The second temptation took place 450 feet above the Kidron Valley, above the temple floor. Jesus was standing on the pinnacle of the temple with Satan. Josephus, the Jewish historian, said this particular place was so high one got dizzy just looking down.

The references to the temple and the holy city are very important in this temptation. According to rabbinic tradition, the coming of the Messiah would be marked by His appearance on the temple roof. If Jesus had jumped off the pinnacle of the temple and landed on the temple floor unhurt, He would certainly have been identified by most of the Jewish people as the Messiah.[9]

Satan was saying, "If You won't work a miracle Yourself, let God do a miracle for You. Jump off and let God catch You and protect You on the way down. That will prove to everyone that You are the Messiah."

In the first temptation, Satan was trying to get Christ to distrust His Father, to be *independent* and make His own bread. In the second temptation, Satan was trying to get Christ to be *presumptuous* and jump from the temple so that His Father would be forced to step in and give Him a smooth landing to protect His plan of redemption.

The devil wanted Christ to set Himself up as a wonder-worker, to put on a show. But the Lord had the perfect sword ready. He said, "It is written again, 'You shall not tempt the LORD your God'" (Matt. 4:7). Here Jesus overcame Satan's temptation by quoting Deuteronomy 6:16.

If you have a tendency to be presumptuous with God—to demand from Him things He hasn't promised—remember this saying: "It is absolutely right to believe in miracles; it is absolutely wrong to schedule them."

Did you notice that when Satan tempted Jesus the second time, he quoted the Bible himself? He said, "It is written: 'He shall give His angels charge over you,' and 'in their hands they shall bear you up, lest you dash your foot against a stone'" (Matt. 4:6). That is from Psalm 91:11–12.

Satan knows God's words, and he's not above using them to his advantage. He uses Scripture to lead us to question God, or by selectively using Scripture, he tries to confuse us, as he tried to do to Christ in this temptation. Yes, as the psalm says, God will give His angels charge over us. He will bear us up. But the scripture Satan chose to ignore was the very one Jesus thrust back at him: "You shall not tempt the LORD your God" (Deut. 6:16). Satan's deception is clever, and he will use anything, even the Word of God, to try to trick you.

The selective misuse of Scripture reminds me of the story of a professed Christian who became involved in a bitter feud with a neighbor. He wanted to get rid of the man but considered himself too devout to do it overtly. So he decided to use Scripture. He wrote to his enemy, "The Bible says that Judas 'went and hanged himself' (Matt. 27:5). It also says, 'Go and do likewise' (Luke 10:37). And finally, we read, 'What you do, do quickly' (John 13:27)."

I've heard it said that you can prove anything if you're willing to twist Scripture tightly enough. That is one of Satan's favorite tactics.

THE PRIDE OF LIFE

Matthew 4:8–9: "Again, the devil took Him up on an exceedingly high mountain, and showed Him all the kingdoms of the world and their glory. And he said to Him, 'All these things I will give You if You will fall down and worship me.'"

The devil is the ruler of this world (John 14:30). He usurped that title from humanity when Adam and Eve sinned in Eden. When he faced Jesus in the wilderness, Satan offered to turn over to Him the entire world as His own kingdom to rule. The only catch was that Jesus would have to acknowledge Satan as His master. In other words, he tempted Jesus with personal ambition—with pride.

Jesus came into the world for the very purpose of setting up a worldwide kingdom. But standing dark and ominous in the path to that goal was the cross. So the devil offered Jesus a shortcut that would bypass the cross: "Why don't You take this physical, temporal kingdom I offer in place of the kingdom for which You came? Why not avoid the cross and take Your kingdom by force? I can help You do that. Maybe it's not what You originally had in mind, but it will get You to the same place. Surely the end justifies the means."

We can see why this third temptation might have appealed to Jesus much more than the previous ones—because the devil was offering a way of ruling the world without going through the agony of the cross!

Once again Jesus reached into the sheath of swords and pulled out the *rhema* of God: "Away with you, Satan! For it is written, 'You shall worship the LORD your God, and Him only you shall serve'" (Matt. 4:10). Our Lord replied to the third temptation by commanding Satan to leave and emphatically rejecting his offer with a quote from Deuteronomy 6:13.

Now let's notice the concluding statement of this entire temptation sequence as given in Matthew 4:11: "Then the devil left Him, and behold, angels came and ministered to Him."

It happened for Jesus just as James said it will happen for us: "Resist the devil and he will flee from you" (James 4:7).

THE EXECUTION

You have the same access to the same Scripture that Jesus did, which means you can have the same success over temptation that He experienced. Here are three ways to use God's Word to overcome temptation.

STAY IN THE LINE OF FIRE

It's hazardous to go to church if your pastor is a Bible preacher. It's as if he's standing in the pulpit slinging swords in every direction. Some of those swords are going to hit you where you are; they're going to become God's *rhema* to your heart.

Many times throughout my years of preaching, people have come to me after a service to tell me how God touched their life through my sermon. But often when they tell me what God did for them, it had absolutely nothing to do with the plan or purpose of my message. I've scratched my head over this phenomenon many times. Finally I realized the sayings of God may be incidental verses or phrases that I'm hardly aware of, but God uses them to change a person's heart.

People have become Christians through listening to a stewardship message. A woman became a Christian recently at our church through a Christmas message on the genealogy of Jesus Christ. Go figure.

What I am telling you here is that the declaration of a scriptural phrase or word has power we don't realize. Never underestimate the potential of just one sword!

You don't have to be in church to get hit with a sword, because there are so many ways to listen to God's Word—including through electronic devices. I did a little homework on this in preparation for this book:

- The longest chapter in the Bible is Psalm 119. You can listen to its 176 verses in about fifteen minutes.
- You can listen to the book of Hebrews in about forty-five minutes and the book of Romans in about one hour.
- You can listen to the first five books of the Bible (Genesis through Deuteronomy) in about twelve hours.
- You can listen to the entire Bible in seventy-five hours.

Paul gave these instructions to his young friend Timothy: "Until I come, devote yourself to the public reading of Scripture, to preaching and to teaching" (1 Tim. 4:13, NIV). Access to the Scripture is so easy today that we have little excuse for failing to embed it in our hearts.

SEARCH EVERY INCH OF THE ARMORY

Did you notice where the Lord got all three of the swords He used in His encounter with Satan? Every single quotation came from the book of Deuteronomy.

The book of Deuteronomy is one of the most assailed books in the Old Testament, apart from Daniel and Isaiah. Modern scholars have attacked the book's authorship, its position in the canon, and the authenticity of some of its texts. But by quoting exclusively from Deuteronomy in His clash with Satan, it's almost as if Christ looked into the future, saw these attacks coming, and said, "I believe I'll put a little stamp of blessing on that book by pulling My swords out of that room in the armory."

Today it's not just Deuteronomy and a few other Bible books, but the Bible as a whole that's being attacked, questioned, and dismissed by a culture rapidly succumbing to the glittering temptations of modernity. *GQ* magazine recently ran an article titled "21 Books You Don't Have to Read" that listed modern and historical classics they think no longer have value in today's culture. The Bible is on that list.[10]

But just as Jesus affirmed the authenticity of Deuteronomy with His quotes, the Holy Spirit affirms the authenticity of all Scripture. As Paul wrote, "All Scripture is God-breathed and is useful for teaching, rebuking, correcting and training in righteousness" (2 Tim. 3:16, NIV).

The Bible is our armory, and if we're to resist temptation we must develop skill and acumen in handling all of the weapons it provides for us.

START GATHERING YOUR SWORDS

When Professor Ken Berding was a student at Multnomah University, he (among many others) was amazed by one of his professors, Dr. John Mitchell, the founder of the college. In his nineties, Dr. Mitchell still taught classes to students. While his longevity was amazing, there was something else at which his students marveled: the amount of the Bible he had committed to memory. During his classes, Dr. Mitchell hardly needed his printed Bible—he could recite relevant passages word for word. Berding estimates Dr. Mitchell had memorized the entire New Testament and large portions of the Old.

In a conversation with Dr. Mitchell, Berding asked how the professor managed to memorize so many scriptures. Berding remembers this key part of Mitchell's memory program: before preaching or teaching the Bible, he read the section he was focusing on out loud at least fifty times. From there, committing portions to memory came easy. Berding recounts how that insight revolutionized his own commitment and strategy for memorizing God's Word, leading to his own four-step memory plan:

1. Choose portions of Scripture that can be read out loud in about fifteen minutes.
2. Read that portion aloud once or twice a day until you've read it aloud fifty times.
3. Only then begin committing it to memory.
4. Once the passage is committed to memory, quote it from memory at least twenty-five times. Additionally, record your recitation into a recording device (e.g., your smartphone) so you can play and listen to it while driving, exercising, or other times.[11]

You've committed your phone number, address, Social Security number, birthday, and many other personal pieces of information to memory by repetition over the years. Repeating Scripture can produce the same result.

To emphasize the importance of committing Scripture to memory, visualize a different version of the scene we just explored above. Satan has accosted Jesus in the wilderness, and he has just thrust at Jesus his first temptation. Jesus, wanting to respond with Scripture, says, "Could you wait a minute while I get my concordance?"

To imagine Jesus responding in such a way is preposterous, but it's almost as crazy that so many Christians have no better grasp of Scripture than they do. Most temptations that assail me don't come while I'm walking around with a Bible in my hand. That means I need to store up these swords in my mind so that when temptation comes I can call on them to ward off the attack and defeat it.

Charles Swindoll wrote:

> I know of no other single practice in the Christian life more rewarding, practically speaking, than memorizing Scripture. That's right. No other single discipline is more useful and rewarding than this. No other single exercise pays greater spiritual dividends! Your *prayer life* will be strengthened. Your *witnessing* will be sharper and much more effective. Your *counseling* will be in demand. Your *attitudes* and *outlook* will begin to change. Your *mind* will become alert and observant. Your *confidence* and *assurance* will be enhanced. Your *faith* will be solidified.[12]

When we memorize the Bible, we make it portable. It becomes accessible to us day and night. When we open our Bibles, God opens His mouth. And when we memorize what He says, it's like having His voice recorded in our minds, ready for playback at the blink of an eye. Having the words of God at the ready is critical to the Christian life because of what strong temptation does to our minds.

Resisting Satan in our own strength can be futile. He is too strong for us. We cannot overcome the devil or his temptations without the presence of God in our lives.

That's why it's so critical, so necessary, to have scriptures stored in our minds. They are our only consistently effective weapons against our adversary.

Louis-Charles Bourbon, the son of King Louis XVI of France and his wife, Marie Antoinette, was the heir-apparent to the French throne. Born in 1785, Louis-Charles was four years old when the

French Revolution broke out in 1789 and his father was deposed. The royal family was removed from the Versailles palace and imprisoned in Paris.

When his father and mother were guillotined in 1793, eight-year-old Louis-Charles was officially the new king of France—in the eyes of those who remained loyal to the ruling family. But the revolutionaries were determined that he would never rule. Though they held him in prison, they dared not execute him for fear of alienating too many loyalists.

Instead, according to legend, they devised an alternate plan. They would expose the young prince to all kinds of temptations, and when he inevitably succumbed, he would be discredited in the eyes of his supporters. So Louis-Charles was presented with rich foods, hoping to make him a slave of appetite. They exposed him continually to foul language, hoping to corrupt his mind and speech. They surrounded the prince throughout his waking hours with every temptation they could think of to discredit him and drag him into dishonor.

But the boy did not slip or yield to the temptations set before him. Astounded at his resistance, they finally gave up their program and asked him why he never partook of the extreme pleasures constantly dangled before him. The young Louis-Charles replied, "I cannot do what you ask because I was born to be a king."

And this is the most compelling reason for living pure lives in the face of the lure of pleasure, pride, and position that assails us every day. We, too, are born into a kingly family, and we are promised a glorious destiny. As the apostle Paul wrote, "If we endure, we shall also reign with Him" (2 Tim. 2:12).

We were born to be kings and queens. What can any earthly temptation offer in comparison with our glorious destiny in heaven?

To be an Overcomer, set your eyes on Jesus and see Him as the ultimate object behind your deepest desires. Once you develop a real longing to be in His presence, to become one with Him, and to love

Him throughout all eternity, temptation will no longer have any real power over you.

*Your word I have hidden in my heart,
that I might not sin against You.*
—Psalm 119:11

CHAPTER 9

OVERCOMING EVERYTHING WITH PRAYER

I once heard a story about a mother who got a call from school saying her young daughter was ill. She hurried to pick up her child and then called the doctor. But the doctor's schedule was already overbooked that day. He could see the child the following morning, and in the meantime recommended an over-the-counter medicine to ease her symptoms.

The mother tucked her little girl in bed and drove to the pharmacy, bought the medicine, and hurried back to her car, only to realize she'd left her keys in the ignition and locked herself out!

When she called her daughter to explain why it was going to take more time to get home, the little girl told her to find a coat hanger. "Mommy, I've seen it on TV. They stick the coat hanger down inside the window, hook it on the handle, and the door opens."

The mother went back into the store and was able to get a wire coat hanger. She made attempt after attempt to open the car door, with no luck. Finally, she lifted her racing heart to the heavenly Father.

"I don't know what to do, Lord. My keys are locked in the car, my little girl is at home sick, and I'm here with this coat hanger. Lord, please send someone to help me."

As she finished her prayer, a car pulled up at the curb and dropped off a passenger. The man had a rough look, like he hadn't shaved for days, and it occurred to her he might be homeless. But she said to him, "Sir, can you help me?"

"What's the problem?" he said.

"I've locked my keys in the car, and I've got this coat hanger, but I don't know what to do with it."

"Lady, let me have your coat hanger."

After bending the hanger and inserting it down alongside the window glass, he quickly opened the car door.

The mother was so overwhelmed that she threw her arms around the scruffy guy and gave him a hug. "You are such a good man," she told him.

"Lady," he replied, "I'm no good man. I just got out of prison this morning."

As he walked away, the mother lifted her hands up to heaven and prayed again. "Thank You, Lord—You sent me a professional."

God sometimes answers prayers in unexpected ways! In fact, I think He finds great delight in surprising us with His answers. But regardless of how the answer comes, He hears our prayers and responds to them. For this reason, prayer is the overarching key to being an Overcomer.

LEARNING TO PRAY
LIKE AN OVERCOMER

It can be frightening for a pastor to preach or teach on the subject of prayer for a number of reasons. First, the pastor himself may realize he doesn't pray as he should. Second, he's pretty sure most of the people he's preaching to don't pray as they should either.

So, with the understanding that our prayer lives are probably an area we can all improve on, let's join together in this quest. Instead of examining what we don't do, let's look at what we *can* do by the grace of God.

In this chapter, I want to unfold Ephesians 6:18 in seven expanding segments to consider the critical characteristics of prayer that enable us to be Overcomers in our warfare against Satan. In Ephesians 6:10–18, the passage we've explored throughout this book, Paul instructed us to put on the armor of the Lord so that we might stand against the wiles and strategies of the enemy. Now we come to the postscript of this famous section of Scripture: "Praying always with all prayer and supplication in the Spirit, being watchful to this end with all perseverance and supplication for all the saints" (v. 18).

In Ephesians 6, Paul made it clear we're in an ongoing war. Our enemy is Satan, who has usurped our rightful dominion over the earth (Gen. 1:28) and claimed the title of prince of the world. As a result, we who follow God are now part of a resistance movement living in enemy-occupied territory.

But our Lord and Commander is determined to lead us in the struggle to take back what's rightfully ours. This means we're engaged in a titanic battle against invisible powers and principalities determined to cut us off from God and force us to draw on our own meager resources. Prayer is our line of communication—our secret lifeline that connects us to our Leader, giving us His strength and direction every day.

This is why Paul devoted special space to prayer following his discussion of the believer's armor. These implements of warfare are described almost in passing—in a few words or a simple phrase. But then Paul slowed down and gave us a robust doctrine of prayer in twenty-four words.

If you have any doubts about the importance of prayer, please consider its high place in the life and ministry of our Lord. Here is how S. D. Gordon described it:

> Prayer . . . was not only His regular habit, but His resort in every emergency, however slight or serious. When perplexed He prayed. When hard pressed by work He prayed. When hungry for fellowship He found it in prayer. He chose His associates and received His messages upon His knees. If tempted, He prayed. If criticized, He prayed. If fatigued in body or wearied in spirit, He had recourse to His one unfailing habit of prayer. Prayer brought Him unmeasured power at the beginning, and kept the flow unbroken and undiminished. There was no emergency, no difficulty, no necessity, no temptation that would not yield to prayer. . . . How much prayer meant to Jesus![1]

Even though Jesus is no longer physically on the earth, prayer—that is, communication with the Father—is still important to Him. Do you know what He is doing right now in heaven? He is at the right hand of God interceding for us (Rom. 8:34)!

If the Lord Jesus considers it important for Him to pray, and He has been interceding for us at the throne of God for the last two thousand years, maybe those of us who are less than diligent in our prayer life should stop and ask ourselves—are we missing something?

THE PERSISTENCE OF THE OVERCOMER'S PRAYER

"Praying always . . ."

In his letter to the Thessalonians, Paul told the believers in that city to "pray without ceasing" (1 Thess. 5:17). Jesus said it this way: "Men always ought to pray and not lose heart" (Luke 18:1).

What does it mean to "pray always"? Do we walk around like zombies, oblivious to our surroundings, mumbling mantras under our breath? No! It means we're in constant contact with God, like soldiers on the battlefield connected to their commander via radio. This is how we maintain our connection and learn to live in fellowship with Him.

If we live this way, we won't have to begin each prayer with an introductory announcement, like a knock on His door: "Lord, we come into Your presence. . . ." If we live in an attitude of prayer, we're always in His presence.

A vivid example of praying always is the character of Tevye, the struggling Jewish milkman in the classic stage play and film *Fiddler on the Roof.* As Tevye works and interacts with his family and neighbors, he carries on a running conversation with God, chatting with Him like a friend. He talks about whatever comes into his head—his daughters getting married, his lame horse, his poverty, and his dreams. He pauses to carry on business and take care of needs, but the moment those things are done, he's back in conversation with God. It's as if his life is his prayer, and the everyday things he must do are mere islands in the stream that flows continually from his heart to God.

How can you pray always in your life today? One way is to look for triggers—prompts throughout your day that remind you to pray. For example, I read of one man who prayed every morning while brushing his teeth that God would give him wise words to say, and as he washed his face, he asked God for a cheerful countenance.

Today we also have smartphones with prayer apps you can download. You can use your phone to set up "prayer reminders" just as you do an alarm. You can use the calendar-alert function to remind you to "pray the hours," pausing every three hours for a few moments to offer a praise or petition to God.

In fact, any behavior, time, or event can prompt you to pray—if you make it a habit.

"Praying always" also means praying persistently. In Jesus' parable in Luke 11, a man answered a knock on his door late in the night. This was likely a common experience, for in the hot summer climate of Israel, most travel of any distance was done at night. The hungry guest had to be fed, but the host's cupboard was bare. So, he ran to a friend's house, banged on the door, and asked to borrow food.

His friend's family was asleep on their mats. "Go away," the friend replied. "Do you realize what time it is? My door is locked, we're all in bed, and we don't want to be bothered."

Then Jesus thrust home His point:

> But I tell you this—though he won't do it for friendship's sake, if you keep knocking long enough, he will get up and give you whatever you need because of your shameless persistence.
>
> And so I tell you, keep on asking, and you will receive what you ask for. Keep on seeking, and you will find. Keep on knocking, and the door will be opened to you. For everyone who asks, receives. Everyone who seeks, finds. And to everyone who knocks, the door will be opened. (Luke 11:8–10, NLT)

Philip Yancey wrote, "If such a neighbor eventually rouses to give you what you want, how much more will God respond to your bold persistence in prayer! . . . We should pray like a salesman with his foot wedged in the door opening, like a wrestler who has his opponent in a headlock." Yancey concluded by saying, "Raise your voice, Jesus' story implies. Strive on, like the shameless neighbor in the middle of the night. Keep pounding the door."[2]

THE POSSIBILITIES OF THE OVERCOMER'S PRAYER

"Praying . . . with all prayer . . ."

For such a tiny word, the term *all* has an expansive meaning. It means everything that can be placed in the basket. No limits. No exclusions. The entire gamut. The whole enchilada. Here, describing the word *prayer*, it means every kind of prayer you can think of.

But Paul goes further. He tells us there's nothing that cannot be prayed for and no situation in which prayer is not helpful.

Stuart Briscoe wrote, "When our children were small and we were trying to teach them to pray, we had three kinds of prayer: 'Please prayers,' 'Thank you prayers,' and 'Sorry prayers.'"[3]

Into those kinds of prayers—prayers of petition, prayers of thanksgiving, and prayers of confession—can fit every time, place, and need that you have.

PRAY ON ALL OCCASIONS

Whether you're sitting at a stoplight, waiting at school, seeing the doctor or dentist, doing the laundry, or mowing the lawn—any time you have a spare moment, keep the communication lines open between yourself and the throne of God.

If those occasions sound like they lack the reverence that should accompany prayer, consider when Scripture tells us to pray: when we're thankful (2 Cor. 1:11; Phil. 1:3), when we need to confess a sin (James 5:16), when we're sick (James 5:14), when we're in danger (Acts 27:29), when we're tempted (Matt. 26:41). We should pray at public occasions such as church meetings (Acts 12:5) and in prayer groups (Acts 12:12). We should pray at social and festive occasions such as weddings, parties, or dinners.

PRAY IN ALL PLACES

Today it's common for believers to pray around the dinner table, in Bible classes, at our bedside, while jogging or walking, and in our own personal devotionals. All are great times for prayer!

New Testament people (sometimes the Lord Himself) prayed in the following locations: in a solitary place (Mark 1:35), on a mountain (Matt. 14:23), in the temple (Luke 2:37), on a housetop (Acts 10:9), in a house (Acts 10:30), in the church (Acts 12:5), at a riverside (Acts 16:13), on a ship (Acts 27:29), and in prison (Acts 16:25). Believers are also encouraged to pray in their own rooms (Matt. 6:6) or, as the King James Version says, to pray in a closet.

PRAY AT ALL TIMES

The New Testament records prayers being offered before daylight (Mark 1:35), on the Sabbath day (Acts 16:13), when alone (Luke 9:18), when together (Acts 2:42), all night (Luke 6:12), night and day (1 Tim. 5:5), and continually (Acts 6:4). We're to pray in sickness and in health, and at any hour. There's never a time when we cannot pray.

PRAY FOR ALL THINGS

To make an exhaustive list of what New Testament people prayed for would be—exhausting!

But to name a few, they prayed (or were encouraged to pray) for: safety (Matt. 24:20), forgiveness (Mark 11:25), food (Luke 11:3), faith (Luke 22:32), other people (John 17:9), healing (James 5:14), spiritual wisdom (Eph. 1:17), relief from suffering (James 5:13), rain (James 5:18), children (Luke 1:13), health and prosperity (3 John 1:2), and spiritual strength (Matt. 26:41).

In other words, there are no limits! We should pray for personal things, home things, business things, and work things. *All* things should be covered by prayer. If it's something you're concerned about, it's something you should pray about.

Our goal as Overcomers is to be able to reach out in prayer at any moment and immediately be in touch with God. Our whole life can be a prayer as we walk day by day with Him. Don't sweat the details; leave those to God. Just pray!

THE PETITION OF THE OVERCOMER'S PRAYER

"Praying . . . with . . . supplication . . ."

Supplication means "to ask," as in asking God to provide for our needs. Of course we come to Him with worship and thanksgiving and gratitude, but we also must come asking.

Some Christians think petitionary prayer is a low form of prayer—one that is sometimes necessary, but on the whole is a bit unworthy of a mature, truly spiritual Christian. They see it as centered on self, making us like needy or even greedy children, pestering God with our continually expanding want list.

But the New Testament *encourages* us to offer petitionary prayers.

When Jesus taught His disciples the model prayer to pray, He filled it with requests not only for ideals, such as the advancement of God's kingdom, but also for our daily and personal needs such as food, forgiveness, and deliverance from evil (Matt. 6:9–13).

In the Sermon on the Mount, our Lord invites us to pray petitionary prayers without holding back, and He promises those prayers will be heard and answered. James, the Lord's brother, tells us our failure to place our needs before God explains the lack of power and peace in our lives: "You do not have because you do not ask" (James 4:2).

At this point a natural question arises. Since God is all-powerful and all-knowing, He knows our needs even before we ask. Jesus Himself affirmed this point: "For your Father knows the things you have need of before you ask Him" (Matt. 6:8). But if God already knows our needs better than we do, why do we need to pray at all? Why doesn't God do for us what He knows needs to be done?

There are four answers.

First, we pray to maintain and deepen our connection with God. We're keeping the communication lines intact and operative so we'll know His will.

Second, God wants us to want what He knows we should have. Prayer gets our minds attuned with Him and enables us to see our needs from His perspective. The more we pray, the more we see how our prayers are answered, which draws us closer to the mind of God and improves the effectiveness of our prayers.

E. Stanley Jones puts it this way: "Prayer is surrender—surrender to the will of God and cooperation with that will. If I throw out a boat-hook from the boat and catch hold of the shore and pull, do I pull the shore to me, or do I pull myself to the shore? Prayer is not pulling God to my will, but the aligning of my will to the will of God."[4]

Third, God tells us to pray for our needs so we'll acknowledge Him as the source of all we have. Asking and receiving enhances our awareness of our continual dependence on Him.

Augustine gives us a fourth reason for petitionary prayer: Prayer is preparation. God wants you to pray so that your capacity to receive His gifts might be enlarged.[5]

Charles Spurgeon wrote:

> Asking is the rule of the kingdom. . . . It is a rule that never will be altered in anybody's case. . . . If the royal and divine Son of God cannot be exempted from the rule of asking . . . , you and I cannot expect the rule to be relaxed in our favor. . . . God will bless Elijah and send rain on Israel, but Elijah must pray for it. If the chosen nation is to prosper Samuel must plead for it. If the Jews are to be delivered Daniel must intercede. God will bless Paul, and the

nations shall be converted through him, but Paul must pray. Pray he did without ceasing; his epistles show that he expected nothing except by asking for it.[6]

So, if you don't pray boldly enough to ask for what you need, don't be upset that God isn't working in your life as you wish He would!

THE POWER OF THE OVERCOMER'S PRAYER

"Praying . . . in the Spirit . . ."

What power drives our prayer? It is the power of the Holy Spirit who lives within us. The Holy Spirit within determines the character and the content of our prayer. He directs, shapes, and corrects the prayers of sincere believers who are fully committed to doing God's will.

We need the Holy Spirit's involvement in our prayers because we are fallen. Our sinful nature acts like a blanket of fog, obscuring our awareness of the presence of God. In our present state, the things of God are not completely clear to us. As Paul put it, "For now we see in a mirror, dimly. . . . Now I know in part" (1 Cor. 13:12). Even our best and most sincere efforts at prayer may inadvertently miss the mark of God's will for us.

So how can you know if what you are praying for aligns with the will of God? The Holy Spirit who wrote the Word of God is the same Holy Spirit who lives in your heart. He knows your heart, and He knows the Father's heart, because He is one with the Father. Because of this, He knows your intent when you pray. He takes your fumbling prayers and reshapes them to reveal the deepest needs beneath the surface of your words.

The daughter of a friend of mine played oboe in the sixth-grade beginners band, and my friend was looking forward to their first concert. His neighbor, who also had a daughter in the band, asked, "How can you stand it? All those missed notes, squawking violins, and the whole thing off-key?" My friend replied, "Well, I guess I just hear what they intend!"

When you pray, the Holy Spirit within you knows what you intend.

> Likewise the Spirit also helps in our weaknesses. For we do not know what we should pray for as we ought, but the Spirit Himself makes intercession for us with groanings which cannot be uttered. Now He who searches the hearts knows what the mind of the Spirit is, because He makes intercession for the saints according to the will of God. (Rom. 8:26–27)

Watchman Nee explains the power of prayer like this: "Our prayers lay the track down on which God's power can come. Like a mighty locomotive, his power is irresistible, but it cannot reach us without rails."[7]

Someone observed the following about Peter's escape from prison after the church prayed in Acts 12: "The angel fetched Peter out of prison, but it was prayer [that] fetched the angel."[8] Prayer makes a difference because it has real power.

While Jason Meyer was in graduate school working on his doctorate, he also worked the night shift at UPS to pay the bills. With so much going on, he never got enough sleep. Early one morning, driving home at 4:30 A.M. after his night shift, he struggled to stay awake. He turned up the radio, tried to sing along, slapped himself—anything to stay awake. Suddenly he found himself regaining alertness in his driveway. He had no memory of driving home!

Inside, he expected to find his wife asleep, but she was sitting up in bed, waiting for him. Instead of her usual "How was work?" she asked how his drive had been. He related what a struggle it had been to stay awake and how he couldn't remember most of the drive home, and his wife said, "Yeah, I figured. . . ."

Earlier that morning, at exactly 4:30 A.M., she'd woken up suddenly with the intense sense that she needed to pray for her husband. So she began to pray. Jason Meyer is convinced the Spirit of God woke up his wife specifically to pray him home safely.[9]

THE PRECISION OF THE OVERCOMER'S PRAYER

". . . being watchful . . ."

To be watchful means "to be awake, to be vigilant." For us, it also means being precise in prayer, as we identify and pray for strength to overcome specific challenges.

As Paul transitioned from describing the Christian's armor to the subject of prayer, notice how he retained the military imagery. He did this because we face a very real enemy, which means we must maintain vigilance, stay watchful, and keep guard at all times.

When the Jews returned to rebuild the ruined walls of Jerusalem after the Babylonian captivity, the Samaritans and their allies were determined to stop the construction and attacked the workers. But the Jews held them off by arming the builders and maintaining a red-alert level of vigilance: "Those who built on the wall, and those who carried burdens, loaded themselves so that with one hand they worked at construction, and with the other held a weapon. Every one of the builders had his sword girded at his side as he built" (Neh. 4:17–18).

Like these watchful Jews, you must live your Christian life with a dual focus. Perform your normal tasks and duties for your family, employer, and society—your everyday work that sustains your life and relationships. At the same time, wage a battle against powers intent on destroying you eternally! You can and must attend to both tasks simultaneously.

As one woman prayed, "Dear Father in heaven, so far today I've done pretty well. I haven't gossiped or lost my temper; I haven't been greedy, grumpy, nasty, selfish, or overindulgent. But, God, in a moment I'm going to get out of bed. And from that point on, I'm going to need a lot of help from You."

To be up and awake means the battle is engaged. As an Overcomer, the enemy will attack you with distractions, doubts, and temptations to abandon prayer. Guard your prayer time and keep your prayers constantly flowing. Prioritize prayer as you plan your schedule. Encourage everything that feeds and fosters your prayer life. Focus your prayers as precisely as you can, but if you don't know exactly what to pray for, don't avoid prayer or hesitate to pray. Instead, trust that the intention of your prayer will be heard and understood.

The late E. V. (Ed) Hill's résumé could fill several pages: pastor of Los Angeles Mount Zion Baptist Church, a megachurch and a center of social and political activism; the friend of several presidents and Dr. Martin Luther King Jr.; co-laborer with evangelist Billy Graham; faithful friend to pastors and leaders; one of the first African American preachers to be broadcast weekly over television; a leader in his Baptist denomination . . . and more.

But when E. V. Hill was born into poverty in 1933 in Columbus, Texas, no one predicted his stunning success in life. His Depression-era family was so poor that his mother sent him, at age four, to live with a friend in the nearby community of Sweet Home, Texas. Ed grew up calling this loving woman "Mama."

Although she had very little material means, Mama had big faith and big plans for Ed. Against all odds, Ed graduated from his rural high school—the only member of his graduating class. But that wasn't enough for Mama; she insisted Ed was going to college. After he was accepted at Prairie View A&M University, Mama took Ed to the bus station, handed him a ticket and five dollars, and said, "Mama is going to be praying for you."

On the day he registered for classes, he had $1.90 in his pocket, and he needed $80.00 in cash to register and be admitted. He had no source for that kind of money, but remembering that Mama was praying for him, he got in line anyway. In one ear he heard the devil saying, "Get out of line," and in the other ear he heard Mama saying, "I'll be praying for you." He believed in Mama's promise of prayer and stayed in line.

The closer he got to the front of the line, the more nervous he became. But just as the girl ahead of him finished with her registration and turned to walk away, Ed felt a hand on his shoulder. It was Dr. Drew, an official at the college: "Are you Ed Hill from Sweet Home?" Ed answered that he was. "Have you paid your fees yet?" Ed answered that he had not.

"We've been looking for you all morning," Dr. Drew said. "We have a four-year scholarship for you to cover room and board, tuition, and $35 per month for expenses."

And once again, Ed Hill heard Mama saying, "I'll be praying for you."[10]

Sometimes prayer is our only resource—like when you leave home for college on a bus with five dollars in your pocket.

What do you think Mama was praying for young Ed?

I'm guessing she didn't know precisely what it cost to attend college for four years, but she knew there would be expenses. Perhaps she simply prayed that God would make a way, that God would meet Ed's needs, and that Ed would learn to trust God every step of the way. And she must have kept praying, because after graduating college with a degree in agriculture, Ed was called to his first pastorate in Austin, Texas—the beginning of a life of preaching.

"Continue earnestly in prayer, being vigilant in it with thanksgiving" (Col. 4:2).

THE PERSEVERANCE OF THE OVERCOMER'S PRAYER

"Praying . . . with all perseverance . . ."

If we're not careful, prayer is a habit we can fall into and out of. If you've hit a snag and stopped praying for a little while, don't let it throw you into a tailspin. It's impossible to miss the point of these scriptures:

- "They continued steadfastly in the apostles' doctrine and fellowship, in the breaking of bread, and in prayers" (Acts 2:42).
- "We will give ourselves continually to prayer and to the ministry of the word" (Acts 6:4).
- "Rejoicing in hope, patient in tribulation, continuing steadfastly in prayer" (Rom. 12:12).

Satan often uses two strategies to discourage you from your prayer life. The first, strangely enough, comes through success. If you've experienced two good days of prayer, he'll convince you that your prayer will always be that powerful and clear. "You're a natural!" he'll whisper in your ear.

Then, on the third and fourth days, when the sparks don't ignite and your prayers can't seem to get out of your room, he'll come and say, "Well, now we see who you really are! You may as well give up; there's no use trying anymore."

When you experience what feels like failure, remember that your momentary feelings are never a barometer of your spiritual life. Sometimes when I pray it seems the heavens open and God's presence beams down on me. Other times it feels like my words are leaden and fall heavily to the floor instead of ascending to God. Even so, those "flat" prayers are just as valuable as those that pulse with vibrancy!

Our emotions come and go—strong one day, subdued or absent

the next. They cannot be the standard you use to measure your enduring spiritual connection with God. Remember, we have within us the power of the Holy Spirit, who can lift our prayers to the Father even when they seem too dull to be airborne.

If you feel your prayers aren't feeding you or reaching God, try reading about prayer. When I get cold toward prayer, I read a book on the subject, and it fills my heart with hunger and a desire to pray. Get yourself a good, solid book on prayer and use it in conjunction with the Scripture. Read a little every day, and let God begin to work in your heart and rekindle your desire to pray.

Satan's second strategy to discourage your prayer life is to convince you that prayer doesn't work in general, or that your prayers don't work specifically. For example, if your prayers aren't answered the way you expected, Satan tries to convince you that you're not a good enough Christian to merit God's attention—you don't have enough faith, or you don't have what it takes to live a spiritual life.

But many answers don't come the way we want or expect because God has something better in mind! The crippled man at the temple gate in Acts 3 asked for money, but God—working through Peter and John— gave him healing. Paul asked for healing, but God gave him strength.

To pray effectively is to persevere, no matter how soaring or how earthbound your prayers feel. No matter how focused, failing, or frantic you feel. The more you pray in all circumstances, the more you align your will with God's, which will mean more visible answers.

THE PURPOSE OF THE OVERCOMER'S PRAYER

"Praying . . . for all the saints"

Young men and women enlist in the armed forces for different reasons.

But once they are serving, their dedication to those who serve with them becomes one of their deepest commitments.

So it is in the Christian life as well. Our love for each other becomes a prime motivation for action. This is why Paul urged us to engage in supplication for all the saints.

Jesus set the example when He prayed for His disciples: "I pray for them. I do not pray for the world but for those whom You have given Me, for they are Yours" (John 17:9). Paul regularly prayed for those in the churches he visited, making mention of them always in his prayers (Rom. 1:9; Eph. 1:16). Job's three friends angered God with their presumptuous judgments, but we read "the LORD restored Job's losses when he prayed for his friends" (Job 42:10).

When we pray for one another, everybody in the body of Christ is praying for everybody else in the body. Although I may be praying for you instead of for myself, I don't need to worry about my needs being met because while I'm praying for you, you're praying for me!

Fern Nichols, founder of Moms in Prayer International, tells the story of her husband, Rle, and their ten-year-old son Troy canoeing with a friend and his son on the Fraser River in British Columbia. It was early spring, when the snowcaps melting off the mountains caused the river to run high and rapid. It was also raining that morning, but their friend, who canoed the river in all kinds of weather, insisted there was no danger. Trusting his judgment, they shoved off.

It was mid-afternoon when Fern felt a strong need to pray for her husband and son. She put everything aside and took out her Bible. She prayed for their protection and, from Psalm 125:1–2, for strength to endure whatever they were experiencing: "Those who trust in the LORD are like Mount Zion, which cannot be shaken but endures forever. As the mountains surround Jerusalem, so the LORD surrounds his people both now and forevermore" (NIV). For almost an hour she prayed continually that God would bring them home safely.

Later she learned that at the exact time she was prompted to pray, the four canoers had been propelled into the air over a waterfall and thrown into the icy river. Rle fought his way to the surface, found Troy, and saw the canoe floating some distance away. He said later he didn't know where the strength came from, but holding Troy as high as possible to prevent hypothermia, he managed to swim to the canoe and latch on. The other father and son also found the canoe, but after battling the freezing, raging torrent for forty-five minutes, their strength was giving way when their feet touched the river bottom. They climbed the rise and huddled together against the current, chilled to the bone.

Minutes later they heard the welcome beat of helicopter blades hovering overhead. A couple upriver had seen the disaster and called immediately for help.

After arriving safely home, Rle learned the source of the strength he needed to save his son and endure the freezing water for almost an hour. It was from God, sent to them through the channel of his wife's prayer.[11]

Fern prayed, and God answered. We must do the same. Pray for those who have needs, ask God for His help, thank Him for His provision, and intercede for others as Jesus intercedes for you.

Jesus intercedes for us because He loves us. Can we do any less for those we love?

THE PRACTICE OF THE OVERCOMER'S PRAYER

Are you prepared to pray effectively? Do you feel confident in your ability to pray as you should? If not, don't despair. Prayer is something you can learn.

Professor Donald Whitney of the Southern Baptist Theological Seminary offers excellent advice: "If you've ever learned a foreign language, you know that you learn it best when you actually have to speak it. The same is true with the 'foreign language' of prayer. There are many good resources for learning how to pray, but the best way to learn how to pray is to pray."[12]

The story is told of a great conductor who was walking down a street in Manhattan when someone stopped him and asked how to get to Carnegie Hall. The conductor answered: "Practice, practice, practice."

That's the way it is with prayer. The best preparation for an overcoming spiritual life is to pray, pray, pray.

To be an Overcomer, I urge you to begin an active and regular prayer life. This means setting aside time. It means developing the regular habit of connecting your mind to God in private and on the go. It means getting rid of distractions. It means finding a place where you can pray undisturbed.

After becoming England's prime minister, Winston Churchill grew concerned about the ability of his war cabinet to work effectively if Germany attacked from the air as expected. He wanted to know how the central core of the military could function with six hundred tons of bombs falling all around it. Strategists devised evacuation plans for those in power, but Churchill didn't want to flee London. So another scheme was used. A series of storage rooms beneath the Office of Public Works Building was refitted into a top-secret military command post.

Located between Parliament and Number 10 Downing Street, this building was the strongest structure in the area. Workers reinforced it with additional concrete and installed state-of-the-art systems to make sure unimpeded communication could continue even if London were bombed.

In May 1940, Churchill visited his underground bunker and declared, "This is the room from which I'll direct the war." Pointing a stubby finger at the desk, he added, "And if the invasion takes place, that's where I'll sit—in that chair. And I'll sit there until the Germans are driven back—or they carry me out dead."[13]

For the next five years, these subterranean rooms were the nerve center for the war, their existence a tightly guarded secret. Communication flowed in and out of them in steady currents. From here, Churchill guided the conflict, called Allied leaders, and growled out his famous radio speeches to the nation. From here, he had direct access to the world.

Jesus told us in Matthew 6:6 to enter our "closets" (KJV) and pray to our Father in secret. He was referring to the storage rooms in Israeli homes in the first century. In those days, houses were filled with children and animals, and there was little privacy. But most houses had a room for storing supplies. It would have been a small room, cluttered and unheated. But it was a place where one could find a few moments of peace and quiet for prayer. For the believer, Jesus said, such a humble spot provides direct access into the presence of God Himself. It's a secure communications complex where prayers can be rendered and rewarded.

As you embrace the practice of prayer, you'll find many ways to fill your life with it. Pray in the ways that come naturally, then grow and mature your practice of prayer steadily. Fill your life with the joyful discipline of praying without ceasing. This is how to prepare yourself for communication with your Commander as you engage in life's daily battles. This is a key foundation to life as an Overcomer.

The earnest prayer of a righteous person has great
power and produces wonderful results.
—JAMES 5:16, NLT

CHAPTER 10

OVERCOMING DEATH
WITH LIFE

On April 22, 2018, James Shaw Jr. was sitting with a friend at a Waffle House counter near Nashville, Tennessee, when a gunman wearing only a green jacket opened fire.

Shaw bolted from his seat and slid along the ground as he looked for the gunman. When the shooter paused to reload, Shaw rushed at him.

"I acted in a blink of a second," Shaw said. "When he reloaded his clip, that felt like 30 minutes. I looked at him, and he wasn't looking at me. He just had the barrel down. It was like, 'Do it now. Go now.' I just took off."

He told the *New York Times*, "I was just trying to live. . . . I just wanted to live, and he was, like, astonished, that I wanted to live."

They fought over the weapon for what felt like a minute, Shaw said, until he was able to wrest the rifle away from the shooter and throw it behind the counter. That's when the gunman fled.

It wasn't until Shaw left and got in his truck that he noticed blood dripping from his arm and realized a bullet had grazed him. Doctors later treated his hand for burns from the still hot barrel of the rifle he'd grabbed.

Four innocent lives were lost in that Sunday-morning attack, and four other people were wounded. Law enforcement officials and customers said Mr. Shaw, a twenty-nine-year-old electrician, prevented even greater bloodshed. But James Shaw found the outpouring of gratitude and respect uncomfortable. His response to being called a hero?

"I'd rather you regard me as James, you know, just a regular person," he said. "Because I feel like everybody can do pretty much what I did."

Shaw insists the shooting played out too quickly for him to be a hero. "I know I saved other people. I have a 4-year-old daughter: I didn't even think about her. In the midst of it, I was just trying to save myself."[1]

Like James Shaw, all of us want to live. The drive to survive is our most powerful impulse, hardwired into every fiber of our being. So imagine having the power to avert your own death, and then choosing not to.

THE GREATEST OVERCOMER

I began this book by telling you the story of David, the greatest Overcomer of the Old Testament. I want to conclude it by pointing you toward the greatest Overcomer of all time, the Lord Jesus Christ.

Through Jesus' death, burial, and resurrection, He overcame our greatest enemies: sin, Satan, and death. Jesus overcame these enemies personally, He overcame them powerfully, and most importantly, He overcame them permanently. That is the great message of the gospel.

One of the things I like best about the gospel is how simple it is to understand. We can condense it to a single sentence, such as this famous verse from the apostle Paul: "For the wages of sin is death, but the gift of God is eternal life in Christ Jesus our Lord" (Rom. 6:23).

However, we run into trouble if we present the gospel as simplistic—if we give the impression that it's "normal" or "ordinary" in some way. This "gift of God" isn't ordinary. The resurrection of Jesus Christ represents an epic struggle that deserves our attention and our unending gratitude. The book of Hebrews explains it like this: "Since the children have flesh and blood, he too shared in their humanity so that by his death he might break the power of him who holds the power of death—that is, the devil—and free those who all their lives were held in slavery by their fear of death. . . . For this reason he had to be made like them, fully human in every way" (2:14–17, NIV).

Perhaps you know the essential elements of God's good news, but imagine you were hearing it for the very first time. Ben Patterson helps us do that in his book *Deepening Your Conversation with God*, where he writes of a primitive tribe in the jungles of East Asia who knew nothing of the gospel and who lived in fear of death.

One day a group of missionaries arrived with *The Jesus Film*, which tells the story of Jesus from the gospel of Luke. This 1979 film has been translated into more languages than any other film in history. Hundreds of millions of people have been drawn to Christ through showings of this film. But not only had this tribe never heard the name of Jesus, they'd never even seen a movie before!

"Then, all at once, on one unforgettable evening, they saw it all," wrote Patterson, "the gospel in their own language, visible and real."

The tribe watched this good man, Jesus Christ, heal the sick, bless children, teach multitudes, and perform miracles. They were enthralled. But when Jesus was seized and abused by Roman soldiers, they were outraged. They stood and shouted at the screen. When Jesus continued to suffer, they turned on the missionary operating the projector. Maybe he was responsible for this injustice!

The missionary stopped the film and explained the story wasn't over. The people settled back on the ground, holding their emotions in tenuous check, as the movie projector started where it left off.

But then came the crucifixion. They watched in horror as Jesus was stripped and forced onto the cross. They cried in agony with every hammer blow pounding spikes into His hands. The Lord's suffering was intense, and then He died. That was more than the crowd could endure. They began weeping and wailing with such depths of grief the film had to be stopped again. Once more, the missionary calmed the crowd, promising the story still wasn't over.

Then came the resurrection.

They watched again as they saw the women come to the Lord's tomb, bewildered to find the stone rolled away and the sepulcher empty. In a flash of light, two angels appeared, saying, "Why do you seek the living among the dead? He is not here; He is risen!"

Then came the moment Jesus Himself appeared, draped in white, smiling, and saying, "Peace be with you!"

Pandemonium erupted. Joy swept over the watchers like a wind from heaven—everyone jumped, danced, and celebrated as though they'd just heard the best news in the world, which, of course, they had. The missionary again shut off the projector, but this time he didn't tell them to calm down because they'd just learned the great truth of the gospel—by His death, Jesus broke the power of death, freeing those enslaved by their fear of it.[2]

Oh, I wish I'd been there to see it in person. I would have shouted too!

Those of us who have heard the story of the resurrection all our lives may forget how wondrous and joyous and life-changing it is. But in this chapter, I ask you to keep the resurrection of Jesus Christ fresh in your mind. For it is God's answer to death and His eternal gift to every Overcomer.

THE UNBEARABLE WEIGHT
OF THE FEAR OF DEATH

According to the Bible, our Creator-God is eternal, without beginning or end, existing from everlasting to everlasting (Ps. 90:1–2). He is "the King eternal, immortal, invisible" who created us in His image and placed eternity in our hearts (1 Tim. 1:17; Ecc. 3:11). The reason death creates such fear in our minds is because we were made to live forever!

If you struggle with an unbearable, unmitigated fear of death, you're not alone. Not even among sincere Christians. The fear of death is fixed in each of us instinctively.

Peter Thiel, the billionaire behind PayPal and the first outside investor in Facebook, intends to live to the age of 120. He told the *Washington Post*, "I've always had this really strong sense that death was a terrible, terrible thing."[3]

But with all his wealth, Thiel has no good way of avoiding it. Instead, he intends to put it off as long as possible. In addition to following a strict diet, he reportedly takes human growth hormones, although that comes with risks. "There's always a worry that it increases your cancer risk," Thiel explained, "but I'm hopeful we'll get cancer cured in the next decade."[4]

Thiel isn't the only Silicon Valley entrepreneur to put his mind and money behind a quest for longevity. Larry Ellison, the co-founder of Oracle, invests heavily in life-extension ventures. "I don't understand how someone can be here, then not be here," he said, mystified by the universal reality of death.[5]

Yet another venture capitalist, Bill Maris, is haunted by his father's death from a brain tumor. "My thoughts can turn to dark things when I'm alone," he said. Maris has convinced investors to launch Google's billion-dollar, super-secret effort to cure aging.[6]

Many who fear death are interested in cryogenics, the process of freezing oneself in a vat of liquid nitrogen at the moment of death in the hope of being brought back to life in the future when medical research is more advanced. Worldwide, about 350 people are already frozen, and another 2,000 are signed up to become so when the time comes.[7]

Television celebrity Larry King is among them. He's preoccupied with death and begins each day reading the obituaries in the newspaper. When King was nine, his father died of a sudden heart attack. That event ignited King's death obsession. On his TV program, King frequently asked people what they thought will happen to them when they die. Though he's arranged for his body to be frozen, he thinks the idea is absurd. The people behind it are "all nuts," he says, but at least he'll die with a shred of hope. "Other people have no hope."[8]

BEFORE THERE CAN BE A RESURRECTION, THERE MUST BE A DEATH

Death is not the end for those who accept Jesus Christ as their Savior, for He overcame death and rose again, and through Him we also have the promise of eternal life. But to overcome death, Jesus first had to experience it.

Jesus' death, which took about six hours, was witnessed by thousands. He didn't simply swoon or lapse into a coma. He was as dead as a dead man can be.

The Roman soldiers confirmed this by inspecting His stiffening corpse on the cross—they knew death when they saw it. Since Jewish officials could not tolerate crucifixion victims hanging on crosses on the Sabbath day, Roman soldiers broke the legs of those who were crucified to hasten their deaths. This prevented them from pushing themselves up with their legs to breathe. But when the soldiers came to Jesus, they did not break His legs, for they plainly saw He was already dead (John 19:31–36).

Had you been in Jerusalem that day, you would have seen the Lord's body taken down, wrapped tightly in a shroud, and laid in a tomb. And you would have thought, as even His disciples did, that this burial was the end of the story.

On a Saturday night in 1998, Azita Milanian turned down an invitation to go dancing and instead went for a jog. Along the way, one of her dogs, Tango, stopped to smell and scratch at the dirt on the trail. She went to investigate and saw two feet poking out of the ground. At first she thought it was an animal.

Then she heard the infant cry.

Milanian started digging and found a baby wrapped in a blue towel. Lifting him up into her arms, she cleared dirt from his nose and mouth.

"Please don't die," she said. "I will never leave you. I love you."

She flagged down a passing motorist who contacted the Los Angeles County Sheriff's Department. As she waited for police and paramedics to arrive, Milanian tried to comfort the baby.

"He grabbed my wrist and stopped crying. It was very emotional. What kind of sick human would do something like that? He still had his umbilical cord hanging from his stomach."

The baby's body temperature had fallen to eighty degrees. At the hospital he was treated for severe hypothermia. In time, he made a remarkable recovery—the neonatal medical director at Huntington Memorial Hospital called it "really almost a miracle." Nurses named him "Baby Christian."

In time, the baby was adopted. His parents named him Matthew Christian Whitaker.

When he was seventeen, Matthew learned he was adopted. Eventually he was told how he was found. But none of it changed his feelings about his upbringing.

"I'm here today. I've lived a great life. I was adopted into a great family," Whitaker said. "I couldn't ask my parents for any more."

He doesn't dwell on the person who left him. "If this was your best idea, to leave me here, then thanks, because you weren't mentally fit to raise a child."

Twenty years after she found Baby Christian, Milanian and Whitaker were tearfully and joyously reunited. They shared the stories of their lives since that fateful day, and then Milanian took Whitaker to the hiking trail where she'd found him. Growing quiet and serious, Matthew stared through a chain-link fence at the spot.

"This could have been my grave," he said.

To which his rescuer replied, "You were wanted."[9]

True stories like this get us close to feeling the emotions connected with Jesus' resurrection. But we must remember that Jesus wasn't snatched from death in the nick of time. He actually, physically died. And He remained dead for three days before He rose from death and returned to life.

THE EVIDENCE OF JESUS' RESURRECTION

Few historians deny the existence and death of a man in history named Jesus Christ. And the evidence for His resurrection is also compelling.

The historian Luke said that Jesus "presented Himself alive after His suffering by many infallible proofs" (Acts 1:3). What are these "proofs"? That's important for us to grasp, because faith is not trusting God despite the evidence; it's placing logical trust in something reliable.

THE SOLDIERS

If you had the opportunity to witness Jesus' burial, you'd have seen a contingent of soldiers assigned to guard the Lord's tomb day and night (Matt. 27:63–66).

A Roman guard was a security force of sixteen soldiers, each trained to protect six feet of ground. Four stood immediately in front of what was to be protected. The other twelve slept in a semicircle in front of them. Every four hours, another unit of four was awakened, and those who had been awake went to sleep. This went on around the clock.[10]

To steal the corpse of Jesus, grave robbers would have had to walk over the sleeping soldiers, then get past the alert and well-armed guards. Clearly, the "stolen body" hypothesis is patently absurd, but it was the best "spin" the Lord's critics could concoct in the fog of events around His resurrection (Matt. 28:11–15).

THE SEAL

According to Matthew 27:66, the governor also sent soldiers to secure the tomb with an official seal to prevent anyone from tampering with it. This seal consisted of a cord stretched across the rock and fastened at either end with sealing clay. It was stamped with the official signet of the Roman governor.

For someone to have stolen Jesus' body, they would have had to evade the soldiers and then break the seal, which would have incurred the wrath of the Empire.[11]

THE STONE

If you'd witnessed the scene, you'd also have noticed the giant stone that covered the tomb. Matthew 27:59–60 says, "When Joseph had taken the body, he wrapped it in a clean linen cloth, and laid it in his new tomb which he had hewn out of the rock; and he rolled a large stone against the door of the tomb, and departed."

Mark's account says this stone was extremely large. How could a frightened group of disciples or a dispirited group of women overcome the Roman guards long enough to roll away the stone? Critics have no satisfactory answer.

One of the most interesting books on this subject was written by

English journalist Frank Morison, a skeptic of Christianity who wanted to disprove the resurrection. Morison poured over the evidence, hoping to demonstrate that it was a myth. But not only was he unable to disprove the resurrection, the weight of the evidence convinced him of the truth, and he became a Christian himself. His book *Who Moved the Stone?* became a powerful defense of the resurrection.[12]

Who indeed?

The Lord's tomb was hewn out of solid rock. Jewish tombs typically had entrances four or five feet in height. A sepulcher like this had a groove cut in such a way that its lowest part lay in front of the opening. When the wedge holding the stone was removed, it rolled down the groove and slammed into place. Such a stone could weigh up to two tons, which is why the women coming to the tomb on Sunday morning were so surprised to find it open.

So, who did move the stone? Matthew 28:2 says, "And behold, there was a great earthquake; for an angel of the Lord descended from heaven, and came and rolled back the stone from the door, and sat on it."

THE SEPULCHER

And that brings us to the astonishing discovery that shook Jerusalem on that history-bending day: the empty tomb.

Everyone agrees the tomb was empty, even those who deny the gospel. As Paul said, "This thing was not done in a corner" (Acts 26:26). Thousands of people in Jerusalem for Passover could see for themselves that Joseph of Arimathea's tomb, so recently occupied by the body of Jesus of Nazareth, was now vacant.

Did the disciples steal the body of Jesus to perpetrate a hoax? This seems impossible for two reasons. First, how could they sneak past the guards, move the giant stone, take the body of Jesus, and escape with it at all—much less do so without being noticed and stopped by highly trained soldiers?

Second, the disciples were different people following the resurrection. They didn't act like conspirators but like witnesses. Something had moved and changed them, and they went on to suffer and die for the gospel, enflamed by its truth. The disciples didn't die for something they knew was a hoax; they suffered for the truth because they knew beyond a shadow of a doubt that Jesus had overcome death.

Did the authorities move the Lord's body? That's hard to believe, since the authorities could have produced the corpse and ended the story when the apostles began to proclaim Jesus and the resurrection. The message of the resurrection could not have spread in Jerusalem a single day "if the emptiness of the tomb had not been established as a fact for all concerned."[13]

THE SHROUD

We also have a significant detail given to us in John 20:3–8. After Peter and John heard the rumors of the resurrection, they ran to the tomb. When John leaned over and looked into the grave, he saw something so startling that he did not enter the tomb.

Where the body of Jesus had lain, "there were the graveclothes in the form of a body, slightly caved in and empty—like the empty chrysalis of a caterpillar's cocoon. Seeing that would make a believer out of anybody!"[14] John never got over it. One of the most unforgettable things that stayed in the minds of the disciples was the empty graveclothes—undisturbed in their form and position.

THE SCARS

On the evening of that first Easter, Jesus appeared to His disciples as they hid behind locked doors for fear of the Jewish leaders (John 20:19–23). But one man was missing. The disciple Thomas wasn't there. Later, when he heard the reports, he said he would not believe without personal, tangible proof.

"Unless I see in His hands the print of the nails, and put my finger into the print of the nails, and put my hand into His side, I will not believe," he said (John 20:25).

One week later, the disciples gathered again. This time Thomas was there. According to John 20:26–28, Jesus again appeared in their midst and said, "Peace to you!" Then He said to Thomas, "Reach your finger here, and look at My hands; and reach your hand here, and put it into My side. Do not be unbelieving, but believing."

Thomas's response represents the climax of the gospel of John, as he exclaimed, "My Lord and my God!" The scars of Christ, still visible on His risen and glorified body, provided indisputable proof of His identity. Thomas's doubts vanished forever, and according to our best traditional sources, he became a lifelong missionary who gave his life for the expansion of the church in India.

THE SIGHTINGS

Had you been living in Israel during those days, you may have seen the risen Christ, for some of the "many infallible proofs" of His resurrection involve eyewitness accounts. That's the specific point Luke was making in Acts 1:3: "He also presented Himself alive after His suffering by many infallible proofs, being seen by them during forty days."

We know of approximately a dozen post-resurrection appearances Jesus made; on one occasion five hundred people were present (1 Cor. 15:5–8). Christ appeared to men and women, to groups and individuals, in a house and on a street, to disciples who were sad and to those who were happy, on momentary occasions and those that stretched out over a period of time, in different localities and at different times of day. The variety of His appearances is one reason why those who have studied the resurrection consider it to be so well confirmed.

Albert L. Roper was a prominent Virginia attorney, a graduate of the University of Virginia and its law school, and the mayor of Norfolk.

He once began a legal investigation into the evidence for the resurrection of Christ, asking himself the question: Can any intelligent person accept the resurrection story? After examining the evidence at length, he came away asking a different question: Can any intelligent person deny the weight of this evidence?[15]

IT'S TIME TO LIVE LIKE AN OVERCOMER

Jesus Christ overcame death with life. Our knowledge of Christ's resurrection isn't merely an intellectual exercise. Because He lives, you can live too—in the fullest sense of that word. Because He is alive now and forevermore, He has authority to give life, both eternally and abundantly.

These truths have four profound and highly practical implications.

BECAUSE HE IS RISEN, YOU CAN LIVE A FORGIVEN LIFE

Before His death on the cross, Jesus watched His disciples stumble from one mistake to another, culminating in their desertion and denial of Him.

But somehow all their failures were swallowed up in the empty tomb of Christ. Take Thomas, for example. Had he not messed up and stalked away in bitter unbelief, we wouldn't have his triumphant exclamation of the next week: "My Lord and my God!" As I said, John used those words as the climactic moment of his Gospel, for Jesus can turn our failures into acts of faith and faithfulness.

Jesus does that for you and me, and for those we love. The Bible uses a wonderful phrase in Deuteronomy 23:5 and Nehemiah 13:2: "God turned the curse into a blessing."

If something seems like a curse in your life, subject it to the blazing light of the empty tomb. Give it to the risen Christ. Do you have a memory—perhaps a mistake or regret—that haunts you? Something you'd give anything to turn back the clock to correct?

You don't have to.

Because of the resurrection, our Lord can work all things for our good and His glory. Those who put their trust in His death and resurrection receive free and full forgiveness for all their sin, and He can also redeem our mistakes.

The life of every Christ-follower is a miracle flowing out of the greater miracle of the resurrection of our Lord. The Bible says, "Who is he who overcomes the world, but he who believes that Jesus is the Son of God?" (1 John 5:5).

BECAUSE HE IS RISEN, YOU CAN LIVE A MEANINGFUL LIFE

This was the primary point driven home by the apostle Paul in his great chapter on the resurrection, 1 Corinthians 15. In this long and wonderful chapter, Paul studied the resurrection of Christ from every angle. He ended by saying, "Therefore, my beloved brethren, be steadfast, immovable, always abounding in the work of the Lord, knowing that your labor is not in vain in the Lord" (v. 58).

Because of the resurrection, your work is not in vain. The Lord knows how to infuse you with resurrection energy.

In his book *Just for a Moment I Saw the Light*, writer John Duckworth described a Sunday when he was only three—a day when his dad took him to Mrs. Loeffler's Sunday school class at the First Presbyterian Church of Flushing, New York. John didn't want to go, and he pitched a fit at the door, clinging to his dad's legs for dear life. Mrs. Loeffler came to the rescue, suggesting Mr. Duckworth stand in the back of the room. John finally agreed to sit near the front as long as he could look back and see his dad.

When Mrs. Loeffler set up her flannelgraph board and told that week's Bible story, John listened with interest. He watched the cut-out figures come and go across the board. Someone else was listening, too: his thirty-year-old dad, an agnostic who'd come to church only because his wife had suggested it.

"So there we were," John later wrote, "my father and I, both of us beginners. We were locked in a roomful of light with no escape, the son trapped by the father and the father by the son. We had come to the right place."

They returned to the class the next week, and again John took his small seat near the front and Mr. Duckworth stood at the back of the room.

"Mrs. Loeffler arranged her paper people on the flannel board," recalled John, "and again the Light began to shine."

Then one Sunday Mrs. Loeffler came to the greatest story in the Bible. "God had sent His Son, Jesus, to save people. To save everybody who would believe in Him—thirty-year-old fathers, three-year-old sons. Jesus had died for us, and then had come back to life so we could live forever."

John's dad couldn't escape the power of that story. A few months later, he was ready to step into the Light himself, asking Jesus Christ to be his Savior.

"Not until three years later did Mrs. Loeffler finally learn all that had happened in the back of her Sunday School room," John wrote. "My parents had to tell her the story before we left town—before we drove across the country to my father's first pastorate."[16]

John Duckworth went on to become a writer, editor, and illustrator of Christian books. His life was changed by one woman's faithfulness in sharing the gospel, and he has gone on to change the lives of others. The story continues.

Consider how silently and certainly God used a woman who simply signed up to teach the three-year-old class in her church! At the time she didn't know the impact she'd have, or that her efforts would be as meaningful as they became. Mrs. Loeffler's work was not in vain. God used her beyond anything she could have imagined.

In the same way, we need a living purpose to fuel our lives. According to the *Wall Street Journal*, teens with a sense of purpose do better in school, are more resilient, and are healthier. Sadly, only about 20 percent of teens fit into that category. Eighty percent haven't yet found a strong sense of purpose for their lives.[17]

On the other end of the spectrum, more than ten thousand people in America reach the age of sixty every day. Experts warn most aren't ready to retire because of financial issues and because of life-mission issues. People who retire without an ongoing sense of purpose struggle emotionally, spiritually, and physically.[18]

Without the resurrection of Christ, life is ultimately futile. Even our most heroic and enduring accomplishments have limited lifespans, and nothing of value is perpetual or imperishable. But the resurrection of Christ is a trumpet blast of hope, bringing us endless purpose, meaning, and fulfillment.

BECAUSE HE IS RISEN, YOU CAN LIVE A POWERFUL LIFE

Jesus' resurrection was a display of unimaginable power—and that same power is available in our lives. That's the core message of the book of Ephesians, which ends with the dramatic imagery of our overcoming armor. The beaming light of the empty tomb illuminates every sentence and word in Paul's letter to Ephesus.

For example, listen to this paragraph from Ephesians 1. Better yet, read it aloud:

> I pray that the eyes of your heart may be enlightened in order that you may know the hope to which he has called you, the riches of his glorious inheritance in his holy people, and his incomparably great power for us who believe. *That power is the same as the mighty*

strength he exerted when he raised Christ from the dead. (vv. 18–20,
NIV, emphasis added)

To reverse the process of death was no easy thing. How often, when standing beside the casket of a friend or loved one, have I wished I could snap my fingers and wake them up! To bring Christ from death to life, to resurrect His body from the grave, to restart a stilled heart, to open deceased eyes, to transform a dead body into ageless life—only the omnipotent God can do that.

According to this passage, *the very power that brought Jesus back to life is available to you when you put your trust in Him.* That power is available to change your life, to answer your prayers, to resolve your difficulties, and to guide you through life as you live and serve Him, relying on His overcoming grace.

Jesus is our source of power. How grieved He must feel when He sees us walking around defeated all the time, wallowing in self-pity and despair, tumbling headlong into sinful habits. We fall more than we rise, and we stay down longer than we ought.

But this can change.

We have work to do! We have assignments to undertake each day, whether it's teaching three-year-olds, building houses for the poor, visiting the sick, or pursuing our careers as unto the Lord. Every day is meaningful for Christ followers, and He will strengthen you with His power so you can fulfill the assignments He has given you.

BECAUSE HE IS RISEN, YOU CAN LIVE A NEVER-ENDING LIFE

Finally, because Christ is risen, your death is not final. The Bible says, "Christ is risen from the dead, and has become the firstfruits of those who have fallen asleep" (1 Cor. 15:20). Our Lord's resurrection is the guarantee that those who put their trust in Him will also be resurrected. Jesus Himself declared, "I am the resurrection and the life.

He who believes in Me, though he may die, he shall live. And whoever lives and believes in Me shall never die. Do you believe this?" (John 11:25–26).

Because Jesus triumphed over death and will triumph over evil, we have a certain hope concerning the future.

When I conducted the funeral of my mother—whom I loved dearly and love to this day—I cried. But I didn't become hysterical or fight off feelings of despair. I know where she is, and I know Whom she is with. I know one day, by God's grace, I will see her again. There is hope in the midst of all the hurt.

Ruth Dillow was working at her sewing machine at the National Garment Company on Thursday, February 28, 1991, when she was called to her boss's office. Two somber men in uniform were there to tell her that her youngest son, Pfc. Clayton Carpenter, had been killed by a cluster bomb during Operation Desert Storm.

"I can't begin to describe my grief and shock," she wrote. "It was almost more than I could bear. For three days I wept. For three days I expressed anger and loss. For three days people tried to comfort me, but to no avail because the loss was so great."

Neighbors came with flowers, cakes, and casseroles. Sympathy cards filled the mailbox. Nearby businesses posted signs in honor and memory of her son. But Ruth was inconsolable and couldn't take her eyes off a picture of her boy.

"I kept looking at that picture," she said. "I kept saying, 'No. He can't be dead. This has got to be a mistake.'"

Three days later, the phone rang. The voice on the other end said, "Hi, Mom! This is Clayton!" Ruth froze, fearing someone was playing a cruel hoax on her, but Clayton pleaded with her to listen. "Come on, please believe me, this is me!" he said. He was calling from a hospital in Saudi Arabia, lightly wounded but certainly not dead.

"I couldn't believe it at first," said Ruth. "But then I recognized his voice, and he really was alive. I laughed, I cried, I felt like turning cartwheels, because my son whom I had thought was dead, was really alive."[19]

Can you imagine Ruth Dillow's joy? That is the way we should feel about the resurrection of Jesus Christ!

Surely this is how you would have felt had you been there on that first Easter Sunday. Jesus died and then He defeated death—it was unimaginable, yet undeniable. He overcame the one who held the power of death, the devil, and freed us from our fear of death.

Because of Jesus, we can clothe ourselves with the spiritual armor listed in Ephesians 6 and stand in joyful triumph. Just when it seemed humanity was overcome by death, Satan was overcome by Christ. Doubt was overcome by truth, and grief was overcome by joy.

Jesus said, "These things I have spoken to you, that in Me you may have peace. In the world you will have tribulation; but be of good cheer, I have overcome the world" (John 16:33).

You cannot overcome the tribulations of life without Jesus Christ. With my closing words, I plead with you to open your life to Him. Your decision to be an Overcomer is long overdue.

The Bible says, "If you confess with your mouth the Lord Jesus and believe in your heart that God has raised Him from the dead, you will be saved" (Rom. 10:9). You can do that now, at this moment, by making the most life-changing decision in the world—by asking Jesus Christ to become your Savior and Lord.

Let me suggest a prayer to offer. I urge you to make it your own, and to start living out the truths you've read in this book.

Dear Lord,

I believe You love me and have a plan for my life. I realize I have neglected You, disobeyed You, and been separated from You by my sins. With Your help and by Your grace, I'm willing to turn from my sins and receive Jesus Christ as my Savior. I believe He died for me, and I believe He rose again. Here and now, I receive Your overcoming grace and Your overwhelming power—the very power that raised Christ from the dead. May I live for You from this day and forever. In Jesus' name, amen.

Thanks be to God, who gives us the victory
through our Lord Jesus Christ.
—1 CORINTHIANS 15:57

ACKNOWLEDGMENTS

The gap between what we know and how we apply what we know seems to be widening every year. So many of my generation seem to be content to be hearers of the Word of God and not doers. I have set out to change that with *Overcomer*. And that, more than anything else, explains the unusual way we have approached this subject.

I believe stories are windows into the soul, and this book is full of stories. Stories of men and women who have faced the difficulties of life and have overcome.

Jesus is the one who teaches us the importance of stories. Matthew tells us that "without a parable He did not speak to them" (Matt. 13:34). Jesus took common things that His listeners would have known well and constructed a short story by which He would communicate something His listeners did not know. That is what we have attempted to do with the nearly one hundred stories contained in this book!

I have discovered many of these stories through the many books I read each year and through the routine research that is part of my preaching. But there have many others who have sent me stories to read. Tom Williams, Rob Morgan, and William Kruidenier are great storytellers in their own right, and they have shared some of their treasures with me for the sake of this book. Thank you all, and please keep reading—there is another book coming soon.

This project would not have been possible without my literary partner. Beau Sager, you inspire me every day by your diligence and determination. For you, every word matters, every source is sacred, and every minute of editing and rewriting is taken seriously. You have incredible endurance, and you are the glue that holds all of this together.

This is our second opportunity to work with Jennifer Hansen. What a blessing you have been to us, Jennifer. When you have signed off on a chapter, I allow myself to sign off on that chapter. We all believe that you have made what we do so much better, and we thank you!

I owe a great debt of gratitude to the people who surround me at Turning Point. Diane Sutherland is at the center of that world. She understands the pressures that descend upon our office when we are in the midst of a book project, and she guards my schedule and organizes my life so that I can step back from the normal daily challenges and concentrate on finishing another writing project on time. From all of us in San Diego, and from all of the people you influence around the world through your wonderful communication skills, we say, "Thank you!" Diane, you are really good at what you do!

On the production and publishing side of this project there are also some very special people. I would like to give a shout out to a new partner whom we met for the first time during the writing of this book. Daisy Hutton is our champion at HarperCollins Christian Publishing, and I cannot remember any publisher believing in our Turning Point team like she does. You cannot know what that means to me and to the people with whom I work every day.

On the first page of all of my books, you will see the name Yates & Yates, the literary agency founded by Sealy Yates. Thank you, Sealy, for coordinating the efforts between the Turning Point team and the HarperCollins team. We have all been on the same page more with this book.

My oldest son, David Michael, is the leader of the Turning Point team. We have been working together for more than twenty-five years, and we are enjoying the journey more than ever before. David, I feel so blessed to get to see you and work with you every day.

Anyone who knows anything about Turning Point knows the name Paul Joiner! He is the most creative person I have ever known and every year he takes us to a higher place. The work that you and your team did to promote this book has set a whole new standard of excellence for us all! Wow!

This has been a special year for my wife, Donna, and for me. We have just celebrated our fifty-fifth wedding anniversary. Together we have served our Lord for half a century, and what joy we share together during these days as we clip the coupons off a life invested in the gospel. Donna, I am so blessed to be sharing this life with you.

Finally, to Jesus Christ, the greatest Overcomer of all time, we dedicate this book.

David Jeremiah
San Diego, California
July 25, 2018

NOTES

CHAPTER 1: OVERCOMER

1. Erin Kelly, "The True Story of WWII Medic Desmond Doss Was Too Heroic Even For 'Hacksaw Ridge,'" *All That Is Interesting*, January 7, 2018, http://allthatsinteresting.com/desmond-doss.

2. T. A. Boogaart, as quoted in Tremper Longman and David Garland, *The Expositor's Bible Commentary: 1 Samuel–2 Kings* (Grand Rapids, MI: Zondervan, 2010), 178.

3. Malcolm Gladwell, *David and Goliath: Underdogs, Misfits, and the Art of Battling Giants* (New York, NY: Hachette Book Group, 2013), 7–8.

4. Ibid., 9–10.

5. Ibid., 11.

6. Karl Vaters, "The Man Who Saved the World by Thinking Small: A D-Day Tribute," *Christianity Today*, June 6, 2017, https://www.christianitytoday.com/karl-vaters/2017/june/man-who-saved-world-by-thinking-small-d-day-tribute.html?paging=off.

7. Robert J. Morgan, with Reese Kauffman, *Every Child, Every Nation, Every Day* (Warrenton, MO: CEF Press, 2015), 72–73.

8. Max Lucado, *Facing Your Giants: God Still Does the Impossible* (Nashville, TN: Thomas Nelson, 2006), 8.

9. Ibid., 9.

10. Adapted from James Earl Jones, "James Earl Jones on the Importance of Mentoring," *Guideposts*, June 12, 2017, https://www.guideposts.org /better-living/entertainment/movies-and-tv/guideposts-classics-james -earl-jones-on-the-importance-of.

11. Douglas McGray, "Design Within Reach: A Blind Architect Relearns His Craft," *The Atlantic*, October 2010, https://www.theatlantic.com /magazine/archive/2010/10/design-within-reach/308220/.

12. Margalit Fox, "Dovey Johnson Roundtree, Barrier-Breaking Lawyer, Dies at 104," *New York Times*, May 21, 2018, https://www.nytimes.com /2018/05/21/obituaries/dovey-johnson-roundtree-dead.html.

CHAPTER 2: OVERCOMING WEAKNESS WITH STRENGTH

1. Denny Morrison, "Denny Frank on Cheating Death Twice to Make It Back to the Olympics," *Vice Sports*, January 23, 2018, https://sports.vice .com/en_ca/article/mbpdg8/denny-morrison-on-cheating-death-twice -to-make-it-back-to-the-olympics.

2. See Robert J. Morgan, *Nelson's Complete Book of Stories, Illustrations, and Quotes* (Nashville, TN: Thomas Nelson, 2000), 64–65.

3. Mark Ellis, "92-Year-Old Grandma Stops Attacker with Jesus," *God Reports*, August 14, 2012, http://blog.godreports.com /2012/08/92-year-old-grandma-stops-attacker-with-jesus/.

4. Sarah Kaplan, "Some Birds Are So Stressed by Noise Pollution It Looks Like They Have PTSD," *Washington Post*, January 9, 2018, https://www .washingtonpost.com/news/speaking-of-science/wp/2018/01/09 /some-birds-are-so-stressed-by-noise-pollution-it-looks-like-they -have-ptsd/?utm_term=.e1c069a44fa3.

5. Ken Blanchard and Phil Hodges, *The Servant Leader* (Nashville, TN: Thomas Nelson, 2003), 88.

6. Quoted in *Record of Christian Work, Volume 24*, edited by Alexander McConnell, William Revell Moody, Arthur Percy Fitt (Record of Christian Work Company, 1905), 312.

7. John MacArthur, *The MacArthur New Testament Commentary: 2 Corinthians* (Chicago, IL: Almighty Press, 2003), 405.

8. *More Perfect Illustrations for Every Topic and Occasion* compiled by the editors of PreachingToday.com (Wheaton, IL: Tyndale House Publishers, Inc., 2003), 9.

CHAPTER 3: OVERCOMING FALSEHOOD WITH TRUTH

1. "Great Wall of China Hoax," *Museum of Hoaxes*, accessed June 21, 2018, http://hoaxes.org/archive/permalink/the_great_wall_of_china_hoax/.

2. Stephen J. Dubner and Steven D. Levitt, *Freakanomics: A Rogue Economist Explores the Hidden Side of Everything* (New York, NY: HarperCollins Publishing, 2009), 224–225.

3. Harold A. Bosley, *Sermons on the Psalms*, quoted in Gerald Kennedy, *A Second Reader's Notebook* (New York, NY: Harper & Brothers, 1959), 330.

4. R. C. Sproul, *Enjoying God: Finding Hope in the Attributes of God* (Grand Rapids, MI: Baker Publishing Group, 1995), 181.

5. Brett McCracken, "Five Facets of Our Epistemological Crisis," August 12, 2017, https://www.brettmccracken.com/blog/2017/8/3/five-facets-of-our-epistemological-crisis.

6. Os Guinness, *A Time for Truth: Living Free in a World of Lies, Hype and Spin* (Grand Rapids, MI: Baker Books, 2000), 11–12.

7. John F. Walvoord and Donald K. Campbell, *The Theological Wordbook: The 200 Most Important Theological Terms and Their Relevance for Today* (Nashville, TN: Word Publishing, Inc., 2000), 362.

8. Quoted in Isaac Chotiner, "How to Survive Death Row," *Slate*, March 22, 2018, https://slate.com/news-and-politics/2018/03/how-anthony-ray-hinton-survived-death-row.html.

9. Walvoord and Campbell, *The Theological Wordbook*, 362.

10. Stu Weber, *Spirit Warriors* (Sisters, OR: Multnomah Press, 2001), 166.

11. J. D. Greear, *Not God Enough: Why Your Small God Leads to Big Problems* (Grand Rapids, MI: Zondervan, 2018), 99.

12. James Russell Lowell, "The Present Crisis," Bartleby.com (accessed February 22, 2018), http://www.bartleby.com/102/128.html.

13. Hal Bock, "A Coach for All Seasons," *Spokane-Review*, December 4, 2000, C8.

14. Chip Ingram, "How to Speak the Truth in Love, Part 1," *Living on the Edge with Chip Ingram*, accessed May 31, 2018, https://livingontheedge .org/broadcast/how-to-speak-the-truth-in-love-part-1/weekend-radio.

15. Ibid.

16. Quoted in "A Resolution for the New Year: In the Face of Suffering, Unleash Love," Stephanie Gray, January 4, 2017, https:// loveunleasheslife.com/blog/2017/1/3/a-resolution-for-the-new-year-in -the-face-of-someones-suffering-unleash-your-love-by-stephanie-gray.

17. John Ortberg, *The Me I Want to Be* (Grand Rapids, MI: Zondervan, 2010), 198–99.

18. Mark Buchanan, "Thy Kingdom Come," *CT Pastors*, accessed June 13, 2018, https://www.christianitytoday.com/pastors/2010/spring /thykingdomcome.html.

CHAPTER 4: OVERCOMING EVIL WITH GOOD

1. Rachel Denhollander, "Read Rachael Denhollander's Full Victim Impact Statement About Larry Nassar," *CNN*, January 30, 2018, https:// www.cnn.com/2018/01/24/us/rachael-denhollander-full-statement/.

2. "Righteous," *Merriam-Webster*, accessed May 17, 2018, https:// www.merriam-webster.com/dictionary/righteous.

3. Aleksandr Solzhenitsyn, *The Gulag Archipelago, 1918–1986: An Experiment in Literary Investigation, Volume 1* (Boulder, CO: Westview Press, 1998), 168.

4. James R. Edwards, *The Divine Intruder* (Eugene, OR: Wipf and Stock Publishers, 2017).

5. Erwin Lutzer, *How You Can Be Sure You Will Spend Eternity with God* (Chicago, IL: Moody Publishers, 2015), 67–68.

6. *Perfect Illustrations for Every Topic and Occasion*, by the editors of

PreachingToday.com (Wheaton, IL: Tyndale House Publishers, 2002), 115–16.

7. Charles Swindoll, *Tale of the Tardy Oxcart* (Nashville, TN: W Publishing, 1998), 495.

8. "Virginia Man Pays Taxes with 300,000 Pennies to 'Inconvenience' DMV," *KTLA5*, January 12, 2017, http://ktla.com/2017/01/12 /man-brings-300000-pennies-to-dmv-to-inconvenience-the-state/.

9. Andrew Bagnato, "Essian Pep Talks Take 2 Approaches," *Chicago Tribune*, September 19, 1991, http://articles.chicagotribune.com /1991–09–19/sports/9103110332_1_manager-jim-essian-wrigley -field-cubs.

10. Jay E. Adams, *How to Overcome Evil: A Practical Exposition of Romans 12:41–21* (Phillipsburg, NJ: P&R Publishing, 1977), 92–93.

11. Ken Burns, *Lewis and Clark: The Journey of the Corps of Discovery*, Florentine Films and WETA, Washington, DC, 1997.

12. Tom Berman and Alexa Valiente, "When Feuding with Your Neighbor Over a Fence Gets Out of Hand," *ABC News*, January 1, 2015, http://abcnews.go.com/US/feuding-neighbor-fence-hand /story?id=27884426.

13. William Hendricksen, *Exposition of St. Paul's Epistle to the Romans* (Grand Rapids, MI: Baker Books, 1981), 421.

14. Albert Tomei, "Touching the Heart of a Killer," *New York Times*, March 7, 1997.

15. Adams, *How to Overcome Evil*, 47.

16. John MacArthur, *The MacArthur New Testament Commentary: Romans 9–16* (Chicago, IL: Moody Press, 1994), 203.

17. Summarized from John Perkins, *With Justice for All* (Ventura, CA: Regal Books/GL Publications, 1982), 98–103.

CHAPTER 5: OVERCOMING ANXIETY WITH PEACE

1. Joe Martin, "Ex-Energy Employee Smashes into New Career Path," *Houston Business Journal*, May 31, 2016, https://www.bizjournals.com

/houston/news/2016/05/31/ex-energy-employee-smashes-into-new
-career-path.html.

2. "Facts and Statistics," *Anxiety and Depression Association of America*,
accessed April 17, 2018, https://adaa.org/about-adaa/press-room
/facts-statistics.

3. Amy Ellis Nutt, "Why Kids and Teens May Face Far More
Anxiety These Days," *Washington Post*, May 10, 2018, https://
www.washingtonpost.com/news/to-your-health/wp/2018/05/10
/why-kids-and-teens-may-face-far-more-anxiety-these-days?

4. R. Kent Hughes, *Ephesians: The Mystery of the Body of Christ*
(Wheaton, IL: Crossway Books, 1990), 232.

5. Julian Barnes, *Nothing to Be Frightened Of* (Canada: Vintage Canada,
2009), 1.

6. Lindsey Carlson, "In the Valley of Postpartum Depression,"
Christianity Today, December 28, 2016, https://www.christianitytoday
.com/women/2016/december/in-valley-of-postpartum-depression
-christian-women.html.

7. Sara Thurgood, BS, Daniel M. Avery, MD, and Lloyda Williamson,
MD, "Postpartum Depression (PPD), *American Journal of Clinical
Medicine*, Volume Six, Number Two (Spring 2009), http://www.aapsus
.org/articles/11.pdf.

8. Carlson, "In the Valley of Postpartum Depression."

9. Michael P. Green, *1500 Illustrations for Biblical Preaching* (Grand
Rapids, MI: Baker Books, 1989), 260–61.

10. Dietrich Bonhoeffer, *Prisoner for God: Letters and Papers from Prison*
(New York, NY: The Macmillan Company, 1959), 11.

11. Joseph Stromberg, "7 Things the Most-Highlighted Kindle Passages
Tell Us about American Readers," *Vox*, June 8, 2014, https://
www.vox.com/2014/6/8/5786196/7-things-the-most-highlighted
-kindle-passages-tell-us-about-american.

12. See entry for "Merimnao" at *Bible Hub*, accessed May 16, 2018, http://
biblehub.com/greek/3309.htm.

13. See *The Pastoral Luther: Essays on Martin Luther's Practical Theology*, edited by Timothy J. Wengert (Grand Rapids, MI: William B. Eerdmans Publishing Company, 2009), 94.

14. Mark Batterson, *The Circle Maker Devotions for Kids* (Grand Rapids, MI: Zonderkidz, 2018), Kindle edition.

15. Quoted in *The Advance*, May 10, 1906, 589.

16. Max Lucado, *Anxious for Nothing* (Nashville, TN: HarperCollins Publishers, 2017), 120.

17. Original source unknown.

18. Tommy Nelson, "Anxiety Attack!" *CT Pastors*, accessed May 15, 2018, https://www.christianitytoday.com/pastors/2013/winter/anxiety -attack.html.

19. Ibid.

20. Ibid.

21. Ibid.

22. John Evans, "IB: After Son's Suicide, Rick and Kay Warren Share Suffering, Peace with Church Family," *Illinois Baptist State Association*, August 9, 2013, http://www.ibsa.org /article372480.htm.

23. Rick Warren, "Trust One Day at a Time," *Pastor Rick's Daily Hope*, December 18, 2016, http://pastorrick.com/devotional/english /trust-one-day-at-a-time1.

24. David Jeremiah, *Slaying the Giants in Your Life* (Waco, TX: Word Publishing, 2001), 63.

25. Kim Phuc Phan Thi, "These Bombs Led Me to Christ," *Christianity Today*, April 20, 2018, https://www.christianitytoday.com/ct/2018/may /napalm-girl-kim-phuc-phan-thi-fire-road.html.

CHAPTER 6: OVERCOMING FEAR WITH FAITH

1. Ken Davis, *How to Speak to Youth and Keep Them Awake at the Same Time* (Grand Rapids, MI: Zondervan, 1996), 124–26.

2. C. S. Lewis, *Mere Christianity* (New York, NY: Macmillan, 1956), 109.

3. Klyne Snodgrass, *NIV Application Commentary: Ephesians* (Grand Rapids, MI: Zondervan, 1996), 343.

4. Peter T. O'Brien, *The Pillar New Testament Commentary: The Letter to the Ephesians* (Grand Rapids, MI: Wm. B. Eerdmans Publishing Co., 1999), 480.

5. R. Kent Hughes, *Ephesians* (Wheaton, IL: Crossway Books, 1990), 235–36.

6. Debra Michals, "Marla Runyan," *National Women's History Museum*, accessed May 8, 2018, https://www.womenshistory.org /education-resources/biographies/marla-runyan and Daniel Rodgers, "I Can't See It but I Know It's There," *Sermonsearch*, August 5, 2007, https://www.sermonsearch.com/sermon-outlines/46707/i-cant-see -it-but-i-know-its-there/.

7. "MLK Quote of the Week: Faith Is Taking the First Step . . . ," *The King Center*, February 21, 2013, http://www.thekingcenter.org/blog /mlk-quote-week-faith-taking-first-step.

8. Mark Batterson, *Wild Goose Chase: Reclaim the Adventure of Pursuing God* (Colorado Springs, CO: Multnomah Books, 2008), 79.

9. Ron Dunn, *Faith Crisis: What Faith Isn't and Why It Doesn't Always Do What You Want* (Colorado Springs, CO: Life Journey, 2007), 209.

10. "Nicky's Story," *Nicky Cruz Outreach*, accessed May 9, 2018, http:// nickycruz.org/nickys-story/ and "Nicky Cruz: Salvation in the Jungles of New York," *CBN*, accessed May 9, 2018, http://www1.cbn.com /700club/nicky-cruz-salvation-jungles-new-york.

11. Quoted in Herbert Lockyer, *All the Promises of the Bible* (Grand Rapids, MI: Zondervan, 1962), 268.

12. Ben Patterson, *Waiting: Finding Hope When God Seems Silent* (Downers Grove, IL: InterVarsity Press, 1991), 101–02.

13. Tim Keller, *Walking with God Through Pain and Suffering* (New York, NY: Penguin Group, 2013), 5.

14. Jemar Tisby, "Faith Begins Where You End," June 24, 2013, https:// jemartisby.com/2013/06/24/faith-begins-where-you-end/.

15. Stu Weber, *Spirit Warriors* (Sisters, OR: Multnomah Publishers, 2001), 172.

16. Dietrich Bonhoeffer, *Life Together* (Minneapolis, MN: Fortress Press, 2005), 32.

17. Daniel Ritchie, Danielritchie.org, accessed May 9, 2018.

18. "The End of Slavery," *Stories for Preaching*, accessed April 23, 2018, http://storiesforpreaching.com/the-end-of-slavery/.

19. Dunn, *Faith Crisis*, 35.

20. This story is summarized from a message given by General Charles Krulak at the Wheaton, Illinois, Leadership Prayer Breakfast in October 2000.

CHAPTER 7: OVERCOMING CONFUSION WITH WISDOM

1. Matthew Cox, "Combat Engineer Receives Helmet That Saved His Life in Afghanistan," Military.com, accessed June 15, 2018, https://www.military.com/daily-news/2016/04/20/combat-engineer-receives-helmet-that-saved-his-life-afghanistan.html.

2. Anthony Selvaggio, *A Proverbs Driven Life: Timeless Wisdom for Your Words, Work, Wealth, and Relationships* (Wapwallopen, PA: Shepherd Press, 2011), 14–15.

3. J. I. Packer, *Knowing God* (Downers Grove, IL: InterVarsity Press, 1973), 102–103.

4. William Proctor, *The Templeton Touch* (Conshohocken, PA: The Templeton Press, 2012), 57–58.

5. Sinclair Ferguson, *Grow in Grace* (Colorado Springs, CO: NavPress, 1984), 236–37

6. Tremper Longman III, *Baker Commentary on the Old Testament and Psalms: Proverbs* (Grand Rapids, MI: Baker Academic, 2006), 101.

7. Jim Castelli, editor, *How I Pray: People of Different Religions Share with Us That Most Sacred and Intimate Act of Faith* (New York, NY: Ballentine Books, 2011), 55–56.

8. Thomas Jefferson, *The Writings of Thomas Jefferson, Volume 17* (Washington, DC: The Thomas Jefferson Memorial Association, 1905), 130.

9. A. W. Tozer, *The Pursuit of God* (Harrisburg, PA: Christian Pub. Co., 1948), 17.

10. Lady Julian of Norwich, *Revelations of Divine Love* (London: Metheun, 1911), 12.

11. Sherwood E. Wirt, *A Thirst for God* (Grand Rapids, MI: Zondervan, 1980), 25.

12. John Meacham, *American Gospel: God, the Founding Fathers, and the Making of a Nation* (New York, NY: Random House, 2007), 173.

13. Charles Bridges, *A Modern Study in the Book of Proverbs* (Fenton, MI: Mott Media, 1978), 3.

14. Portions of this chapter were adapted from David Jeremiah, *Wisdom of God* (Milford, MI: Mott Media, Inc.), which is out of print.

CHAPTER 8: OVERCOMING TEMPTATION WITH SCRIPTURE

1. Al Covino, "Winners and Winners" in Jack Canfield, Mark Victor Hansen, Hanoch McCarty, and Meladee McCarty, *A Fourth Course of Chicken Soup for the Soul* (Deerfield Beach, FL: Health Communications, 1997), as reproduced on the Leadership Dynamics website, accessed April 24, 2018, https://www.leadershipdynamics.com.au/keep-fish-back/.

2. "Poisonous Paradise," *Stories for Preaching*, accessed April 24, 2018, http://storiesforpreaching.com/category/sermonillustrations/temptation/.

3. Martha Tarbell, *Tarbell's Teacher's Guide* (New York, NY: Fleming Revell Company, 1919), 387.

4. Warren Wiersbe, *Be Loyal* (Colorado Springs, CO: David C. Cook, 1980), 38.

5. Rob Morgan, *100 Bible Verses Everyone Should Know by Heart* (Nashville, TN: B&H Publishing Group, 2010), 127.

6. John MacArthur, *How to Meet the Enemy: Arming Yourself for Spiritual Warfare* (U.S.A.: Victor Books, 1992), 141.

7. Ray C. Stedman, *Spiritual Warfare: Winning the Daily Battle with Satan* (Portland, OR: Multnomah Press, 1975), 116.

8. Paraphrased from *George MacDonald Anthology*, edited by C. S. Lewis (London: Geoffrey Bles, 1970), 31.

9. Stanley D. Toussaint, *Behold the King: A Study of Matthew* (Portland, OR: Multnomah Press, 1980), 76.

10. "21 Books You Don't Have to Read," *GQ*, April 19, 2018, https://www.gq.com/story/21-books-you-dont-have-to-read?utm_source=Cultural+Commentary&utm_campaign=c89f600b05-Jim%27s+Daily+Article+%281%2F12%2F18%29&utm_medium=email&utm_term=0_51f776a552-c89f600b05-273585089&mc_cid=c89f600b05&mc_eid=10b0d7d666.

11. Kenneth Berding, "The Easiest Way to Memorize the Bible," *BIOLA Magazine*, Spring 2012, http://magazine.biola.edu/article/12-spring/the-easiest-way-to-memorize-the-bible/.

12. Charles R. Swindoll, *Growing Strong in the Seasons of Life* (Grand Rapids, MI: Zondervan, 1983), 61.

CHAPTER 9: OVERCOMING EVERYTHING WITH PRAYER

1. S. D. Gordon, *Quiet Talks on Prayer* (New York, NY: Fleming H. Revell Company, 1904), 233.

2. Philip Yancey, *Prayer* (Grand Rapids, MI: Zondervan, 2006), 145–46.

3. Stuart Briscoe, *Getting into God* (Grand Rapids, MI: Zondervan, 1975), 55.

4. E. Stanley Jones, quoted in R. Kent Hughes, *Liberating Ministry from the Success Syndrome* (Wheaton, Il: Tyndale, 1988), 73.

5. Saint Augustine, *Letters 100–155* (New York, NY: New City Press, 2003), 192.

6. Charles Spurgeon, "Ask and Have," accessed April 13, 2018, http://www.spurgeongems.org/vols28–30/chs1682.pdf.

7. Watchman Nee, *The Collected Works of Watchman Nee* (Anaheim, CA: Living Stream Ministry, 1993), 141.

8. Thomas Watson, *All Things for Good* (Amazon Digital Services LLC, 2011), 17.

9. Jason Meyer, "How to Pray in the Holy Spirit," *Desiring God*, April 13, 2018, https://www.desiringgod.org/articles/how-to-pray-in-the-holy-spirit.

10. Martha Simmons and Frank A. Thomas, eds., *Preaching with Sacred Fire: An Anthology of African American Sermons, 1750 to the Present* (New York, NY: W. W. Norton & Company, 2010), 707–8.

11. Fern Nichols, "The Difference One Prayer Can Make," *Faith Gateway*, September 10, 2013, http://www.faithgateway.com/difference-one -prayer-can-make/#.Wu4jAi-ZPm2.

12. Donald Whitney, *Spiritual Disciplines for the Christian Life* (Colorado Springs, CO: NavPress, 2014), 85.

13. James Leasor, *What Went on Behind the Closed Doors of the Cabinet War Rooms* (UK: House of Stratus, 2001), 56.

CHAPTER 10: OVERCOMING DEATH WITH LIFE

1. Alan Binder, "'I Just Wanted to Live,' Says Man Who Wrested Rifle from Waffle House Gunman," *New York Times*, April 23, 2018, https://www.nytimes.com/2018/04/23/us/waffle-house-hero-james-shaw.html.

2. Ben Patterson, *Deepening Your Conversation with God: Learning to Love to Pray* (Bloomington, MN: Bethany House Publishers, 2001), 85–86.

3. Ariana Eunjung Cha, "Peter Thiel's Quest to Find the Key to Eternal Life," *Washington Post*, April 3, 2015, www.washingtonpost.com /business/on-leadership/peter-thiels-life-goal-to-extend-our-time -on-this-earth/2015/04/03/b7a1779c-4814-11e4-891d-713f052086a0 _story.html?noredirect=on&utm_term=.e2053bd5bf58.

4. Bloomberg News, "Investor Peter Thiel Planning to Live 120 Years," *Bloomberg*, December 18, 2014, https://www.bloomberg.com/news /articles/2014-12-18/investor-peter-thiel-planning-to-live-120-years.

5. W. Harry Fortuna, "Seeking Eternal Life, Silicon Valley Is Solving for Death," *Quartz,* November 8, 2017, https://qz.com/1123164 /seeking-eternal-life-silicon-valley-is-solving-for-death/.

6. Ibid.

7. Harry Pettit, "First Human Frozen by Cryogenics Could Be Brought Back to Life in 'Just Ten Years,' Claims Expert," *Daily Mail*, January 15, 2018, www.dailymail.co.uk/sciencetech/article-5270257/Cryogenics -corpses-brought-10-years.html.

8. Mark Leibovich, "Larry King Is Preparing for the Final Cancellation," *New York Times*, August 26, 2015, https://www.nytimes.com /2015/08/30/magazine/larry-king-is-preparing-for-the-final -cancellation.html.

9. Brittany Mejia, "While Out for a Jog, She Discovered a Baby Buried Alive. Twenty Years Later, They Reunite," *Los Angeles Times*, May 18, 2018, http://www.latimes.com/local/california/la-me-ln-baby -christian-20180516-story.html.

10. Josh McDowell and Sean McDowell, *Evidence for the Resurrection* (Grand Rapids, MI: Baker Books, 2009), Kindle location 2534–2539.

11. Ibid., Kindle location 2592.

12. Robert Morgan, "Why I Preach the Literal Resurrection of Jesus Christ from the Grave—1 Corinthians 15," used with permission.

13. Cited in Wolfhart Pannenberg, translated by Lewis L. Wilkins and Duane A. Priebe, *Jesus—God and Man* (Philadelphia, PA: The Westminster Press, 1977), 100.

14. McDowell and McDowell, *Evidence for the Resurrection*, Kindle location 2735-2741.

15. Albert L. Roper, *Did Jesus Rise From the Dead?* (Grand Rapids, MI: Zondervan Publishing House, 1965), see Foreword. Used with permission from Robert Morgan.

16. John Duckworth, *Just for a Moment I Saw the Light* (Wheaton, IL: Victor Books, 1994), 11–17.

17. Clare Ansberry, "Why Teens Need a Sense of Purpose," *Wall Street*

Journal, February 10, 2018, https://www.wsj.com/articles/why-teens
-need-a-sense-of-purpose-1518264001.

18. Jim Davis, "With 10,000 a Day Reaching Age 60, WSU Institute to Seek
Answers," *Herald Net*, September 1, 2017, https://www.heraldnet.com
/business/with-10000-a-day-reaching-age-60-wsu-institute-to-seek
-answers/.

19. Rex Yancey, "Rejoicing in the Resurrection," *Sermon Search*, accessed
June 8, 2018, www.sermonsearch.com/sermon-outlines/24792
/rejoicing-in-the-resurrection/ and Karen S. Schneider, "For the
Parents of a Soldier Reported Killed in the Gulf, Death Takes a
Holiday," *People Magazine*, March 18, 1991, http://people.com/archive
/for-the-parents-of-a-soldier-reported-killed-in-the-gulf-death-takes
-a-holiday-vol-35-no-10/.

ABOUT THE AUTHOR

David Jeremiah is the founder of Turning Point, an international ministry committed to providing Christians with sound Bible teaching through radio and television, the Internet, live events, and resource materials and books. He is the author of more than fifty books, including *A Life Beyond Amazing, Is This the End?, The Spiritual Warfare Answer Book, David Jeremiah Morning and Evening Devotions, Airship Genesis Kids Study Bible*, and *The Jeremiah Study Bible*.

Dr. Jeremiah serves as the senior pastor of Shadow Mountain Community Church in San Diego, California, where he resides with his wife, Donna. They have four grown children and twelve grandchildren.

stay connected to the teaching series of
DR. DAVID JEREMIAH

. . . .

Publishing | Radio | Television | Online

SHARE YOUR
OVERCOMER STORY

· · · · · · · · ·

God is at work every day helping His people be Overcomers. Perhaps He has helped you in a specific way to overcome an emotional, physical or spiritual obstacle in your life. As you study this material, please consider sharing your Overcomer story with us.

Visit www.DavidJeremiah.org/Story to submit your story of how God helped you overcome a difficult situation or how Dr. Jeremiah's teaching in this book has helped you be an Overcomer. We can't wait to rejoice with you in the knowledge that our God gives us the power to live a victorious life.

Submit your story online at www.DavidJeremiah.org/Story

OVERCOMER SMALL-GROUP CURRICULUM

· · · · · · · · ·

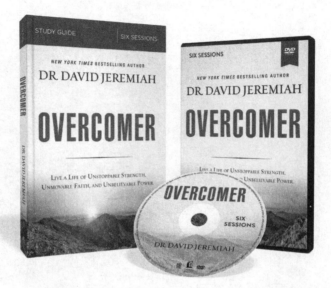

In this six-session Bible study, bestselling author Dr. David Jeremiah turns his insights to one of the most quoted but least understood passages of the Bible: the apostle Paul's admonition in Ephesians 6:10-18 to take up the whole armor of God.

With his signature depth, wisdom, and compassion, Dr. Jeremiah explores the powerful relevance of spiritual armor as a critical tool as we confront the challenges in our daily lives. He reveals how God has given us, His followers, the tools we need to live a life of victory and be Overcomers.

THOMAS NELSON
® Since 1798

FURTHER YOUR STUDY OF THIS BOOK

• • • • • • • •

Overcomer Resource Materials

To enhance your study on this important topic, we recommend the correlating audio message album, study guide, and DVD messages from the *Overcomer* series.

Audio Message Album

The material found in this book originated from messages presented by Dr. David Jeremiah at Shadow Mountain Community Church where he serves as senior pastor. These eleven messages are conveniently packaged in an accessible audio album.

Study Guide

This 144-page study guide correlates with the messages from the *Overcomer* series by Dr. Jeremiah. Each lesson provides an outline, an overview, and group and personal application questions for each topic.

DVD Message Presentations

Watch Dr. Jeremiah deliver the *Overcomer* original messages in this special DVD collection.

To order these products, call us at 1-800-947-1993
or visit us online at www.DavidJeremiah.org.

ALSO AVAILABLE FROM
DAVID JEREMIAH

• • • • • • • •

A Life Beyond Amazing
by Dr. David Jeremiah

Everyone wants to live a life that is beyond amazing. But oftentimes, Christians believe an exceptional life can only be manifested once we are in heaven. But that is not true! God wants us to live an incredible life here on earth! After Christ ascended to heaven, He sent His Spirit to reside in us—giving us these divine traits so that we might live an extraordinary life. Paul called these traits "the fruit of the Spirit" (Galatians 5:22-23).

In this book, Dr. Jeremiah takes us through nine steps, based on Paul's words in Galatians, and breaks down how we can apply each attribute to our daily lives. In doing this, we can live the fulfilling life God has called us to live. If you are feeling like your walk with Christ isn't all that it could be, make the decision to fully pursue a life with God—and live in the blessings that come with it!

To order this book, call us at 1-800-947-1993
or visit us online at www.DavidJeremiah.org.

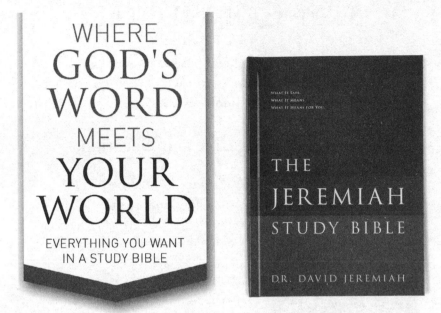

STAY CONNECTED

• • • • • • • •

Take advantage of two great ways to let
Dr. David Jeremiah give you spiritual direction every day!
Both are absolutely free!

① *Turning Points* Magazine and Devotional

each magazine features:

- A monthly study focus
- 48 pages of life-changing reading
- Relevant articles
- Special features
- Devotional readings for each day of the month
- Bible study resource offers
- Live event schedule
- Radio & television information

② Your Daily Turning Point E-Devotional

Start your day off right! Receive a daily e-devotional from Dr. Jeremiah that will strengthen your walk with God and encourage you to live the authentic Christian life.

Request your devotions today:

CALL: (800) 947-1993

CLICK: DavidJeremiah.org/Magazine

Books Written by David Jeremiah

. . . .

Escape the Coming Night
Count It All Joy
The Handwriting on the Wall
Invasion of Other Gods
Angels—Who They Are and How They Help...What the Bible Reveals
The Joy of Encouragement
Prayer—The Great Adventure
Overcoming Loneliness
God in You
Until Christ Returns
Stories of Hope
Slaying the Giants in Your Life
My Heart's Desire
Sanctuary
The Things That Matter
The Prayer Matrix
31 Days to Happiness—Searching for Heaven on Earth
When Your World Falls Apart
Turning Points
Discover Paradise
Captured by Grace
Grace Givers
Why the Nativity?
Signs of Life
Life-Changing Moments with God
Hopeful Parenting
1 Minute a Day—Instant Inspiration for the Busy Life
Grandparenting—Faith That Survives Generations
In the Words of David Jeremiah
What in the World Is Going On?
The Sovereign and the Suffering
The 12 Ways of Christmas
What to Do When You Don't Know What to Do

Living with Confidence in a Chaotic World

The Prophecy Answer Book

The Coming Economic Armageddon

Pathways, Your Daily Walk with God

What the Bible Says About Love, Marriage, and Sex

I Never Thought I'd See the Day

Journey, Your Daily Adventure with God

The Unchanging Word of God

God Loves You: He Always Has–He Always Will

Discovery, Experiencing God's Word Day by Day

What Are You Afraid Of?

Destination, Your Journey with God

Answers to Questions About Heaven

Answers to Questions About Spiritual Warfare

Answers to Questions About Adversity

Quest—Seeking God Daily

The Upward Call

Ten Questions Christians are Asking

Understanding the 66 Books of the Bible

A.D.—The Revolution That Changed the World

Agents of the Apocalypse

Agents of Babylon

Reset—Ten Steps to Spiritual Renewal

People Are Asking … Is This the End?

Hope for Today

Hope—An Anchor for Life

30 Days of Prayer

Revealing the Mysteries of Heaven

Greater Purpose

The God You May Not Know

To order these books, call us at 1-800-947-1993 or
visit us online at www.DavidJeremiah.org.